PRAISE FOR *BECOM*

"*Become an Accelerator Leader* is a joy to read and a valuable guide for every established or aspiring leader. Alvin's storytelling skills reinforce important leadership lessons in a practical way, and he provides clear actionable items to become an accelerator leader. I've known Alvin for many years; he is a person I look up to. I admire his transformative leadership style that accelerates others and creates an abundance of good. I think that's the kind of leader we all want to be."

—Doug McMillon, President and C.E.O. Walmart, Inc.

"Alvin reminds me of my grandfather on so many of the qualities that made my grandfather the leader he was. Alvin has not only been a friend, but a mentor. I am excited that many more will have the opportunity to share in his mentorship through this book. I truly admire his ability to lead with such humility. I am assured that it will accelerate many people's lives positively, thus creating the next generation of remarkable leaders."

—Swati Dlamini Mandela

"Alvin Rohrs is truly one of the most remarkable leaders I have ever met. His natural skill, combined with his ability and willingness to learn from some of the finest business leaders in American history, has made Alvin a potent force for free enterprise. What he created at Enactus is truly remarkable, and the lives of thousands have directly benefited from what Alvin has done. This is the book that many of us urged Alvin to write and I highly recommend it."

—*Matt Blunt, 54th Governor of Missouri; President, American Automotive Policy Council*

"This is a wonderful book that gives leadership advice that is relevant around the world. I have seen firsthand my friend Alvin's accelerator leadership in action in India and globally. In this book, Alvin uses his world-class storytelling ability to share valuable leadership advice. It is fun and inspiring to read. I especially enjoyed his stories from his experiences in nature."

—*Ravi Kant, President, Tata Motors (Retired)*

"You can become an Accelerator Leader and Dr. Alvin Rohrs can show you how!

A superb leadership guide, thoughtfully crafted, by a proven leader and master storyteller who has walked a mile in your shoes."

—*Douglas R. Conant, Former Chairman of Avon Products, Former President and CEO of Campbell Soup Company, NYT Bestselling Author*

"As a student of humanity, Alvin has been blessed with many valuable personal and business experiences. Through his engaging and humble storytelling, he provides a comprehensive expression of the lessons he has learned and guides us to become accelerator leaders. I've listened to many of Alvin's inspirational speeches at Enactus events, and this book is written in the same voice with which he speaks. It serves as a true reflection of a man who wants each of us to achieve our very best."

—*Meg Schmitz, Franchise Development Consultant, "The Franchise Guru", The Wall Street Journal*

"*Become an Accelerator Leader* is a must read for any student of leadership, regardless of experience. It serves as a practical how-to guide for those wishing to lead an organization to new heights and drive change and adaptability. Weaving advice from widely recognized business leaders with tales of everyday situations ranging from fishing to international travel, Rohrs provides a framework that allows the reader to understand complex business concepts with clarity and ease.

"*Become an Accelerator Leader* would be valuable not only as a textbook for most introductory undergraduate leadership courses or classes offered in variable settings, it would also serve as great ancillary material for undergraduate and graduate leadership classes, and in applied entrepreneurial settings."

—*Dr. Robert Wyatt, President, Coker University*

BECOME AN
ACCELERATOR LEADER

Accelerate Yourself, Others, and Your Organization to Maximize Impact

BECOME AN
ACCELERATOR LEADER

**Accelerate Yourself, Others, and
Your Organization to Maximize Impact**

DR. ALVIN ROHRS

gatekeeper press

Columbus, Ohio

Become an Accelerator Leader

Published by Gatekeeper Press
2167 Stringtown Rd, Suite 109
Columbus, OH 43123-2989
www.GatekeeperPress.com

ISBN (hardcover): 9781642375060
ISBN (paperback): 9781642375053
eISBN: 9781642375046
Library of Congress Control Number: 2019930663

Printed in the United States of America

CONTENTS

ACKNOWLEDGEMENTS

My single greatest accomplishment was convincing Elizabeth to marry me. At the time of the proposal, I was such a poor college student that the proposal came without a ring. She said yes anyway. The ring didn't come until Christmas a year later and it had only a diamond chip in it. Our first home was a 10 foot X 50 foot mobile home built the same year she was born. I borrowed $1,500 from her father and mother, Kenneth and Jacky, to buy it and moved it from one trailer park to another. The morning after the first rain in our new home, we discovered that the roof leaked badly. I went to the local hardware store, bought a bucket of roofing tar and climbed on top of the house to give it a new coat. We were in law school and she was already learning divorce law, but didn't use it against me and stayed. The next year, we sold the trailer house for $2,000 and gave it all to my in-laws. I was happy to give them such a good return on their investment.

Elizabeth is now an Associate Circuit Judge in our home county. She was the first woman to practice law in the county; the first woman to be appointed municipal judge in our town; and the first woman to be elected as a county judge. She had three opponents in the election, all men, and she got more votes than all of them combined. Serving as a judge, I have heard her described as having the patience of Job and the wisdom of Solomon. While I spent my career traveling the country and world she spent her time making our community better. She took on leadership roles in Rotary, our church and the P.E.O. sisterhood. She served on the Community Concert and Cemetery Boards and volunteered thousands of hours in many other ways. She has the gifts of hospitality and generosity and uses them often. She makes Rachel Ray look like an amateur. She is a great cook and homemaker and makes a mean blackberry pie from the wild blackberries on our farm. She is an amazing person, an incredible role model and a Godly woman. She is a wonderful wife and mother. I did eventually replace her original engagement ring with one she deserves.

My second biggest accomplishment is being the father of Benjamin and Jaclyn. They are two amazing people. They have their mother's intelligence and good looks and my curly hair. Being part of their life and helping them grow up has been my greatest joy. Watching them mature as adults and find their own ways in life has been a wonderful, scary journey. A perfect day for me is having them back home to visit, with the four of us hanging out around the house and farm, doing whatever comes to mind.

Many of my heroes, mentors, coaches and guides are mentioned in this book. However, there have been far too many people who helped shape my life to mention them all individually. To my extended family, friends, teachers, and even my critics, who have helped me grow, I say "Thank you."

Writing and publishing this book has been a much bigger task than envisioned at the start. My friend and coach, Ellen Langas, owner of Nousoma Communications, kept encouraging, helping and pushing me until I finally got it across the finish line. Thanks!

My most important decision was to commit my life to God and become a follower of Jesus Christ. Without my family and my faith, my life's journey would have been meaningless and impossible.

PROLOGUE

5:00 p.m. September 30, 2016. I am standing on the stage at the Enactus World Cup in Toronto, Canada, for the Final Awards Ceremony. My role is to introduce the staff from around the world, announce the winner of the Country Leader of the Year Award, and make a few comments. I had done this at every Enactus World Cup since 2001, but this one was different. It would be my last time to be on stage as the CEO of Enactus after 34 years in that role.

When I announced, "Country staff, please come forward," I was filled with emotion as they poured out of the audience and came toward the stage. I surveyed the crowd. Over 2,000 students who had spent the year using entrepreneurial action to improve over 2 million people's lives represented over 70,000 students in 36 countries who had done the same thing that year. In total, over 800,000 students had helped over 18,000,000 people during my 34 years. I saw the hundreds of professors and academic leaders who had mentored these students. I looked at the judges – over 500 business leaders, including global CEOs and amazing entrepreneurs.

Then I remembered those who weren't there any longer. Dear friends who had helped us in good times and bad in the early days and recent days; Sonny Davis, the founder; Robert Plaster, my first board member; Jack Shewmaker, our first elected chairman; Sam Walton, our cheerleader; Tony "Too Tall" Stebbins, a past chairman; Ralph Buckingham, one of our first donors; and James Sells, my mentor and boss who green-lighted me to become CEO of Enactus while still on the payroll at Southwest Baptist University.

I was filled with pride.

As the country staff filled the stage, I thought of their many professional and personal struggles: sleeping in the office because of riots in the street, dragging wounded protestors into their apartments during political upheaval in their countries, the loss of children and spouses and parents. One even had a broken jaw and broken ribs because he refused to pay bribes. Yet, through it all, they stayed the course. Looking into the audience, I also saw the faculty advisors who represented the thousands of advisors around the world. These academics were the heart and soul of the organization. They dedicated their careers to developing entrepreneurial action leaders.

I was now filled with humility.

The reality hit me that, while I might have been the architect to move this organization forward for 34 years, it was all of these dedicated people on stage and in the auditorium and in our history who had truly built this organization, and I was putting the future of the organization in their hands when I retired. It was not just the hands of the new CEO, but the hands of thousands of people who were members of this amazing global community who were committed to improving people's lives through entrepreneurial action.

At 12:01 p.m., one minute past midnight, October 1, 2016, I was no longer the CEO of Enactus, and it was okay.

CHAPTER ONE

WHAT IS AN ACCELERATOR LEADER?

There I was, staring at my computer, starting to write something. Many of my friends had said, "You should write a book." What kind? A leadership book, an autobiography, a collection of stories? The consensus was that it should be a book about leadership, based on what I had learned from my experience and from my exposure to so many great leaders.

This day marked the first day home after stepping down from my 34-year career as CEO of Enactus, a global nonprofit that I took the helm of when the organization and I were both fledglings. Both held promise and energy. Both were green. It was like being given a blank notebook and asked to transform it into a powerful novel. As I stared at the computer, I couldn't get started because I wasn't sure what I should call myself in this story. My mind raced. I wasn't the founder of the organization, but I was the architect who grew it into a sustainable global organization with significant impact in 36 countries.

Today I should be content with a job well done. But I couldn't seem to ignore that nagging question, *How should I describe what I did and who I was?*

Across the room in my office/man cave, my collection of Indy 500 memorabilia caught my eye. I started to remember how I helped my late father check off one of his bucket list experiences. My father, Wayne Allen Rohrs, was a racing fan and a bit of a car nut. As a farm boy during the Depression, he had earned enough money to buy a hotrod convertible Mercury and had done a little unofficial drag racing. His car was a 1943 and 1944. They had taken the front end of a 1943 that had been hit in the rear end, and the back of a 1944 that had crashed its front end and welded them together to make a 1943/44 Mercury hot-rod.

Growing up, we watched the Indy 500 every year on TV. We knew the drivers, the cars, and the history. Every year my father said, "Someday I want to go see it live." When I told this to my friend Robert Campbell, an executive with the Valvoline Company, he made it happen. He got us tickets, a hotel room, and gave us VIP treatment, including pit passes the day before the race.

My dad wandered all over the pit area as much as was allowed. He was like a kid in a candy store and had a grin locked on his face all day. The day of the race lived up to its billing: "The Greatest Spectacle in Racing." There were thousands and thousands of fans, media from all over, and food and booze everywhere. We found our great seats courtesy of Robert and felt the excitement as the opening parade began. The cars came out, lined up in race order as determined by a month of time trials. Then, the famous words, "Gentlemen, start your engines" boomed over the loudspeakers.

The 36 cars lit up and roared, just as I had watched for years on TV. I'd heard those words, and I'd heard the engines start for years, but only through the speakers of a TV. There was no lid on this live, in-person noise, and the sound of those engines was so high-pitched and so strong, you could feel the sound waves hitting your body. The green flag dropped and the cars roared through the first turn. They all went into high throttle and slammed on the accelerator, and the sound was even more stunning than I had imagined. It was only seconds before they were back across the starting line. Two hundred miles an hour is fast—too fast to read the numbers on the cars as they speed by. You could barely identify the color of the vehicle. It was much different than watching on TV. That amount of acceleration and thrust is something you can't imagine unless you've personally experienced it. The grin didn't leave my dad's face for a month.

As I sat remembering this amazing experience; how lucky I was to give that gift to my father; and reflecting on the 34-year incredible race I had just finished, it hit me. I may not have been the founder, but I had accelerated my organization from a small regional program to a global impact powerhouse. I was the Accelerator. I had not only accelerated the impact of the organization, but I'd also accelerated the impact of thousands of leaders who had been engaged with Enactus.

I also remembered the early years of my journey and how I had moved at such a rapid pace that I often hit the wall and crashed and burned. How do you accelerate but not hit the wall?

A few years ago, I saw a photograph of Air Force One and its F16 fighter escorts taken on September 11, 2001. That day was unlike any other day and the escort was unlike any other escort. Instead of being thousands of feet above Air Force One, the four F16s were flying extremely close on the tail, left wing, right wing, and nose. It looked like they were almost touching Air Force One. Colonel Daniel Shewmaker, my dear friend, was the pilot leading the squadron flying at the nose.

It is an honor to be Daniel's friend, and I told him so. Then I asked him what it was like flying escort that day and if he was nervous or worried. He responded, "Not nervous and not worried. When you're a fighter pilot you learn to fly calm and steady no matter how fast your plane is going or what's happening around you. We are trained to achieve situational awareness. We train and practice over and over under every possible scenario we can think of to prepare us for taking on those challenges even we could not imagine."

I thought, "Wow, that's what I need to learn. How to stay calm and in control flying at 1,000 miles per hour while making rapid movements to dodge bullets, shoot bullets, and fire missiles." Fighter pilots accelerate more than any other human beings, but the best of them, the career pilots, do it with a calm, steady hand.

Then I remembered watching an Indy car race the first time the TV network had some of the drivers put on heart rate monitors. The announcers were all excited about this new approach to feeling what drivers felt. The cars lined up. No heart rate change. The cars did the warm up lap. No heart rate change. The green flag was waved and the engines roared. No heart rate change. The first turn. No change. The next three turns. No change. The announcers were so disappointed. After a few laps there was a wreck. The announcers said, "Here we go. We will see how this affects the drivers." For the drivers not in the wreck, no heart rate change. For the drivers in the wreck, a very slight uptick that soon went back to normal once their cars stopped flying through the air. These drivers had also learned situational awareness from thousands of laps in hundreds of races. If you are going to freak out going into a turn or getting in a wreck you will wash out of car racing very early. The pros in Indy car racing were calm with steady hands even in the crisis of a wreck.

My conversation with Daniel also reminded me of the 4 million miles I spent on airplanes in my career. Inside a pressurized cabin, all the passengers can move around like they're still on the ground while the plane is moving at 500 MPH in air temperatures well below freezing. It made me consider how I accelerated the people around me and my organization so that their journey is like being in the cabin rather than outside holding onto the wings, fighting the freezing wind with no oxygen.

This book is a guide to becoming an Accelerator Leader. It's about having the greatest impact you can with the time you have.

An Accelerator Leader accelerates his or her own impact, the impact of others, and the impact of his or her organization with peace of mind and a calm, steady hand.

In my journey there were times when the plane was going 500 mph and everyone was inside the cabin moving around as if they were on the ground. There were times when everyone was in their seats with the seatbelt sign on, experiencing turbulence. There were a few times when we were all buckled in our seats in the crash position and I was anxiously pulling us out of a dive. I learned to become an Accelerator Leader from experiences I got right and from those I got wrong. I also had the blessing of learning most of what I learned from great Accelerator Leaders along the journey. This book is a collection of those lessons. If you feel like you're hanging onto the wings outside the plane instead of flying inside the cabin, read on and learn how to *Become an Accelerator Leader* who moves at the speed of a fighter jet, but has the control of a fighter pilot.

SUMMARY:

☞ An Accelerator Leader accelerates his or her own impact, the impact of others, and the impact of his or her organization with peace of mind and a calm, steady hand.

ACTION STEPS:

☞ Determine whether you want to *Become an Accelerator Leader.*

PART ONE

ACCELERATE YOURSELF

———————————————————————

*To be an Accelerator Leader, you must
first be the pilot of your life, your
family, your career . . . everything
that makes you who you are.*

CHAPTER TWO

DETERMINE YOUR DESTINATION; START WITH THE END IN MIND. ENVISION YOUR LEGACY.

KNOW WHERE YOU ARE GOING BEFORE YOU PRESS THE ACCELERATOR

I was hosting an executive retreat that included recreational activities away from a main resort property. I was the driver who took people back and forth from one of these off-site locations. After a fun afternoon, we all piled in the car and headed back to the resort. As often happened at such events, we'd been having so much fun that we were running late. This was in the hills of South Carolina, and there were many winding roads. We came to a "T" in the road and I turned on my right turn signal.

The CEO in the passenger seat said, "No, this is a left." I looked at my pre-GPS directions and it was clear this was a right turn. "I'm pretty sure this is a right," I replied, "What do the rest of you think?"

The passenger riding shotgun was the CEO of a very large division of a very large company. Most of the passengers in the back of the van were his suppliers. Most were CEOs, and all were very senior executives. They knew I was correct, but not one of them said a word. "Turn left!" my shotgunner CEO directed. I thought, if he is this adamant, maybe he's right, so I turned left.

We drove for miles and did not come to the next highway in the directions. We were now very late for the dinner where our shotgunner was to be the speaker. I drove faster and faster, but still no intersection. Then the lights and sirens of a South Carolina state trooper came rolling up behind me. I pulled over and he came to my window to inform me of how much I was going over the speed limit. It was a lot.

While he was writing my ticket, I asked him how to get to our resort. His response was, "Mister, you're heading in the wrong direction. Actually, you need to go in the opposite direction. No matter how hard you push that accelerator you will never get where you want to go."

> *Before you hit the accelerator, you must first know where you are going and determine how you will get there.*

START WITH THE END IN MIND. ENVISION YOUR LEGACY.

Who do you want to become? What kind of impact do you want to make? Who will be there to celebrate when you reach the mountaintop or cross the next finish line?

Your life is like a winding road that you build one mile at a time. Your legacy will be reflected in its hills and valleys, and its ultimate destination. There are three parts of the road: the roadbed that serves as the foundation (you), the pavement that enables the journey (your impact), and the shoulder that provides extra room in an emergency or crisis (the people in your circle of trust). Throughout your lifetime, many people may cross the pavement, some just passing through for a few miles, and some remaining with you to the end of the road. But at the end, it will be those individuals whom you've impacted and nurtured along the way and those whom you have supported in tough times who will celebrate with you. Pay attention to the road you pave, for it will serve as your legacy.

How do you want to be remembered? No matter how young or old you may be, this is where you should start. It may sound a bit morbid, but visualize your funeral and write your own obituary. I live in a rural community where, in the words of singer Miranda Lambert, "Everyone dies famous in a small town," are true. Almost everyone in our town believes in an eternal afterlife, so funerals are quite often celebrations of life and more of a *"see you later"* than farewell forever. As a result, you learn a lot about a person's life at his or her funeral. I am always an observer of life, and this includes when I'm at funerals.

Recently I attended a funeral for Bill Grant, who was a very successful businessman in our town. The main room at the funeral chapel was filled to capacity, and some people had to watch the service on monitors in other rooms. The gathering included current employees, past employees, customers, and community and church friends. The crowd was composed of every socioeconomic level of our community. The deceased had owned a dairy farm and a car dealership and was known for fair deals and friendly service. He measured success in customers for life, not cars sold. His service was a celebration of a life well lived, from the conversations in the hall, to the testimonies of his family and friends, to the songs sung by a gospel duet who happened to be his neighbors. It was a warm funeral on a cold winter day.

The opposite was true of a funeral I attended several years ago where I was to officially represent the organization I worked for at the time. A very small group gathered, and everyone there was an employee, customer, or a charity recipient of the deceased's company. Everyone was there out of a sense of obligation, hoping to be included in his estate, but not because of any affection for this person. No former employees attended. His family was there out of a sense of obligation, or to protect their shares of the estate. I think some attended to make sure the person was really dead and wouldn't come after them anymore. It was almost like Ebenezer Scrooge's funeral scene from *A Christmas Carol*. There were nice words spoken of his great career success and even about how he gave to the community (though most there were thinking he didn't give as much as he should have). No friends or family spoke of fun times or good times they had shared. There was no laughter, only sorrow. He was known as a tough businessman. Tough on his customers, suppliers, employees, and his family. It was a cold funeral on a warm summer day.

What will your funeral be like? What will be said about who you were as a person? What will be said about your impact – how you made the world better than you found it? Will it be a celebration of a life well lived or a formality that puts a period on the end of your life? Who will be there to celebrate you when you cross that final finish line?

As you start with the end in mind, envision your legacy.

SUMMARY:

- ☞ Before you hit the accelerator, you must first know where you are going and determine how you will get there.
- ☞ Your legacy is a winding road you build one mile at a time. Who are you? What impact have you had? And who will join your celebration when you reach the top of the mountain or cross the finish line?
- ☞ As you start with the end in mind, envision your legacy.

ACTION STEPS:

↪ Write your eulogy and include a description of your legacy. Who do you want to be? Who do you want at your memorial service?

CHAPTER THREE

DEFINE YOUR CORE VALUES.

Throughout our lives, competition is all around us. During my career, I have had the privilege of traveling to 40 countries. In those travels, I've spent much time people-watching, and I think I may have learned the most from observing children at play. I have seen children in slums and palaces. In these very different settings, their play eventually involves some form of competition. Who could run the fastest, jump the highest, kick the ball the furthest, or carry the biggest load? It's universal that we have all been wired to compete, and we've been doing it naturally since childhood.

So how does that competitive spirit hurt us or help us as we grow? During my career, I've met people of great success and little success, and I have come to believe that **the most important competition, the one that truly defines success, is the competition between the you that you are**

today and the you that you know you can become. As you strive to win this competition, you will discover that you'll then be able to maximize the impact you make in your world and you'll attract good people who will want to be there to celebrate your success. To win the most important competition, start with the end in mind.

ARE YOU HEADING IN THE RIGHT DIRECTION NOW?

Know who you truly want to be before you hit the accelerator. **If you develop a clear picture of who you want to become and make that your destination, you can chart a course to get there.** You can use that goal to set your compass to true north throughout your life. If your path leads you to become the person you want to be, then accelerate yourself in that direction. If it leads you away from who you want to be, stop and recalibrate!

HOW DO YOU DEFINE THE PERSON YOU CAN BECOME?

This is not about what you look like, how fit you are, or what you do or have done in your career. It's about your character and characteristics. It's about your reputation. It's the real you when you're all alone and looking inside yourself. I have friends who are very successful and very wealthy who hate themselves. They hate the way they gained their wealth; the way they treated others; and some hate the fact that their own family has left them all alone. It's been said that it's lonely at the top, but be assured, it's especially lonely at the top when you're the only one there, and you hate the one person at the top—yourself.

Consider how you want to be remembered. Doing so will better equip you to accelerate in the right direction and make the biggest impact.

DEFINE YOUR CORE VALUES. THEY INCLUDE CHARACTER AND CHARACTERISTICS THAT MAKE UP YOUR REPUTATION.

In the Ozarks, where I live, there are many great outdoor recreation areas and some very remote places to hike and camp. One practice at these remote campsites is for each camper to leave firewood for the next camper to get his or her first fire started. When you arrive at the camp, you can immediately determine the character of the last camper. If there is little to no firewood, that person is a user. They used what the last camper left and didn't have the courtesy to refill what they used. They are making things worse than when they found it. If the firewood is replenished, you know the last camper was a placeholder. "I got firewood, so I will leave firewood. Fair is fair." They pass through life only replacing what they used, making no real difference. If the woodpile is full and overflowing, you know the last camper was a giver. "I was given the gift of firewood and I'll give back an abundance of firewood, just in case the next person can't or doesn't leave any for the future."

This experience tells a lot about a person's character and his or her characteristics. **When you move on to your next location or end your career, will those coming behind you see your character as being a user, a place-holder, or a giver? What will your reputation be?**

Decide what your core values are. In this context, I am defining "character" as those core values that you do not want to compromise. These are issues of ethics and morality. I am defining "characteristics" as those values or issues you choose to be known for, but which are not really issues of right or wrong. Combined, your character and characteristics create your reputation.

CHARACTER IS IN YOUR CONTROL.

As you think about how your reputation will define your legacy, **focus on controlling what you *can* control.** Life is like sailing. As the expression goes, you cannot determine the direction of the wind, but you can control how you trim the sails. No matter what destination you set, life happens. Winds will shift, currents will change, and people will disappoint. Most of what happens to you will be out of your control. What job you get or promotion you receive is never totally in your control. Influence yes, control no.

Integrity. One definition of integrity is, "Being who you say you are and doing what you say you will do." **You cannot control how much truth others speak, but you can control whether you speak the clear truth, the sort-of truth, or an outright lie.**

No one is perfect at always telling the truth, but people around you soon learn whether or not you're a straight shooter. For me, integrity is number one. I often shared with my team that life is like the poster about sailing. You can take many hits above the waterline, patch the holes, and keep on sailing. But if you take one hit under the waterline, you're sunk.

For me, integrity is the water-line. In my work at Enactus, academic competitions were part of our core competencies and methodology. Integrity meant making sure that every competition was judged fairly and accurately. I was often asked who I wanted to win, and my response was always the same: "I don't care who wins; I only care that the process is fair and accurate." Unfortunately, I had to learn from mistakes that being fair and accurate meant controlling the process leading up to the competition as well as the competition itself.

"Your entry material got put into the wrong competition or lost in the mail," is a sorry excuse to a hardworking competitor. Sloppy procedures can lead to breaches of integrity, so you must be ever vigilant. The importance of this became very real as we expanded internationally. Too often we were told, "We will choose our own national winners the way we want to, using our customs."

Our answer was the same: "Every country uses the same judging criteria and competition rules; judging is done in the open." In the short run, there were some countries who did not want to join our work and left, but in the end, sticking to our integrity increased the number of countries that wanted to join. It was a major selling feature to college students in countries who wanted to be part of a competition that was not tainted by corruption.

Two of my favorite definitions of integrity are as follows:

- J.V. Wommack, the "Monument Man" of Bolivar, Missouri said, "You can never go wrong by doing what is right."
- Doug McMillon, the CEO of Walmart, also said it well: "Don't do anything at work you can't go home and tell your children you did."

When I met Len Roberts, he was the CEO of Arby's where he was leading a major turnaround. This turnaround was getting lots of press, especially because of the diversity of the senior management team Len had recruited. Over 50 percent were women or people of color. The turnaround success was a wonderful testament to the strength of diversity in management.

Len was then recruited to be the CEO of Shoney's Inc.. In 1989, Shoney's was considered one of the most successful family restaurant companies in the world. Its multibillion-dollar enterprise operated over 1800 restaurants. But the company was having serious EEOC issues and there was a class action suit filed for racial discrimination. Founder and CEO Ray Danner had abruptly resigned.

Because of those issues, it was no surprise in the industry when Len was aggressively and successfully recruited by the Shoney's board to become its new CEO.

Soon after coming on board, Len realized that this company needed far more than "enlightened management." The company operated for decades with a culture of systematic racism.

As later documented in the book *The Black O,* Ray Danner fired white managers who hired blacks, and instituted such racist practices as having managers blacken the "o" in the word "Shoney's" on job applications to indicate if the form was from a minority applicant so that they would be bypassed for any job considerations.

Ray Danner's store tours were notorious, especially for their overt racism. If he walked in a store and saw too many black employees, he would yell out to the manager that "the coffee is too dark in here and needs to be lightened up."

Danner would always follow up within a week on these targeted store visits, and if the "coffee was not lightened up," the manager was fired on the spot.

Some managers were able to save their jobs by hiding black employees in the store freezers during these follow-up store visits. They knew that Danner hated the cold and never went into the freezers.

The Danner way of leadership went so far as matching contributions made by senior executives to the Ku Klux Klan.

After three years with Len Roberts at the helm of Shoney's, the board was quite pleased with his leadership. The company's performance was far exceeding plan, and the shareholders were being handsomely rewarded.

What the board of directors did not support was Len's insistence that Ray Danner was guilty of discrimination and that the company (or Ray Danner, personally) needed to settle the potential billion-dollar exposure involving over 100,000 members of the class.

The board also did not support Len's direct involvement with Shoney's long-tenured suppliers.

Len was insisting that the suppliers show definitive proof of their commitment to diversity. Many of these suppliers were personal friends of Ray Danner and of the board members.

You can imagine the phone calls to the board members when Len wrote to a number of large suppliers, "If you are going to supply this company in the future, you are going to behave like it's the 1990s and not the 1950s."

Needless to say, many suppliers were changed. To make this policy very clear, Len recruited Betty Marshal, an African American, to be Executive Vice President of Purchasing.

As a public company CEO, Len felt strongly that he had a fiduciary responsibility to protect the assets of the corporation for its shareholders. Therefore, this class action case needed to be settled with a comprehensive consent decree and not tried in a court. The financial exposure was far too great.

The evidence in the case was overwhelming that the actions of Ray Danner and his management team were clear violations of Title VII of the Civil Rights Act of 1964 and of section 1981 of the U. S code.

The quintessential class action issue was straightforward. "Did Shoney's maintain and implement a direct and overt policy of discrimination against African Americans by limiting their job opportunities and by retaliating against white managers who opposed or refused to implement this policy?"

To Len, the answer was clear. And it was equally clear that Ray Danner needed to pay for the settlement personally, and not hurt the innocent shareholders of this public corporation.

The board did not support Len, so he went after Danner by himself. In Len's words, "It was lonely. But I had the support of my wife and my family. And that meant the world to me."

After conferring with the company's lawyers and meeting with the plaintiffs' attorneys, Len had a better perspective of what dollar amount would settle this case: $100-$150 million. Even at the low end, this settlement would be the largest of its type in US history.

Len met with Ray Danner at his home. As Len tells it, "I am sure he thought it was simply another important update on this class action suit. What I proceeded to do in the next 90 minutes was to methodically lay out all the company's own damaging evidence against Ray and Shoney's, including never-before-seen photos of Ray proudly getting dressed in his KKK outfit."

"In Danner's many depositions and in his comments to the media, he always denied that he was a racist and claimed that any disparaging remarks he may have made about any black employee was purely motivated by his intense care for his customers.

"However, the evidence and the photos that I shared with him clearly proved otherwise. And he knew it!

"He was fuming. If he had a weapon handy, I really believe he would have used it on me that evening at his home.

"In the process of his own security personnel physically throwing me out of his home, I was able to effectively lay out my ultimatum, which was clearly within my authority as CEO of the company.

"I told Ray that if I did not have his signed commitment and funds for $130 million within 24 hours to settle this case, I was going to authorize Shoney's Inc. to actually join with the class action plaintiffs in their suit against him and share with them all the damaging evidence I just presented to him."

At seven o'clock the next morning, the lead director of the board called Len and told him that Ray Danner had conditionally agreed to fund the entire settlement. The board wanted to meet with Len that morning to go over Danner's conditions.

The primary condition for Danner to sign the agreement and for the board to approve it was for Len to resign as CEO. Len had just saved the corporation from a billion-dollar exposure and a media nightmare that could have tanked the entire business. He should have been congratulated by the board, not asked to leave.

Len accepted the condition and resigned, and Danner's signed settlement commitment for $130 million was accepted by the plaintiffs' attorneys and ultimately the court.

Len could have refused to resign and gone to battle, but he knew it could destroy the company and cost the jobs of all the employees for whom he had fought. He did what was right for the company and its employees but it was not the best thing for Len, who was now unemployed.

Even though Len left, the leadership team he developed continued his work to change the company culture. Now when I eat at Shoney's, I notice the diversity of the employees and the diversity of the customers and it makes me feel good that I know the integrity of one person can make a huge difference.

Several months after Len resigned from Shoney's he was recruited to head up RadioShack at the Tandy Corporation. He led another turnaround there, was subsequently named Chairman and CEO of Tandy Corporation, and retired after 13 years when RadioShack was at its peak.

Respect others. How you treat others defines you, whether you know it or not. Jack Shewmaker was a great leader and a great mentor of mine. He was the Vice Chairman and CFO of Walmart when we met, and he'd also been the President of Walmart under Sam Walton. He agreed to become the chairman of the nonprofit known as Students in Free Enterprise (SIFE), which is now named Enactus.

As Chairman of the Board of Enactus, Jack was kind enough to share his calendar with me so that when he traveled to any given city, he could work in an opportunity to gather potential supporters and tell them about the organization. This could be a breakfast, lunch, dinner, or reception, anything that would fit in the schedule but didn't interfere with his business for Walmart.

After the first few of these events, I realized that Jack made sure he knew everyone in the room, and I mean everyone: the servers, the busboys, and the head waiter. He shook their hands, called them by name (they wore name badges) and treated them like he did all the top business leaders in the room.

We held our national competition in the same city and hotel for several years while Jack was chairman. Over the years he got to know the headwaiter so well that Jack provided a scholarship for the headwaiter's daughter. Jack was also known as a tough boss. He expected excellence and demanded results. He had little patience for those who didn't carry their load. He was tough but fair.

How you treat others will be a big part of your legacy. Do you "treat others as you would have them treat you?" This sounds easy, but it gets rather complicated in the execution. What does "treat others as you want to be treated" mean to you?

Trustworthiness is a characteristic that is totally in your control, but totally determined by others. You know if you are honest and telling the truth. But, being seen as trustworthy is totally up to others. As Covington covers very well in his book, *The Eighth Habit*, "Trust is a function of character and competence." Do you have the character people will trust, and do you have the skills needed to be trusted to do a specific task?

You control the character issues: can you keep a confidence? Are you reliable and honest? You also control the skills you possess and the knowledge of what those skills can accomplish. Part of being trustworthy is having the character to admit that you don't have the skills to be trusted with a specific task or to be very clear about what your skill levels are. "I think I can do this, but you need to know..." is much better than saying, "I've got this" when you really don't have the skills needed. The rest is up to others to deem you trustworthy.

Loyalty seems to be a value in decline when you look at work tenure, but I'm not sure seniority is the best measure of loyalty either. I remember standing in the office of one of my former college professors. It was a brand-new office in a brand-new building. His old office had been in a very old house converted haphazardly into an office building. It was damp and cold all winter and scorching hot in the summer and had few windows. The walls were paper thin, so confidential conversations never happened. I asked him, "How do you like your new digs?"

His response was, "The windows are too big." I saw that he had covered them with a bookcase full of books. I then remembered that when I was his student, he was always complaining about the school administration or the dean or the other faculty. He could tell you the exact number of days, weeks, months, and years to the date he would retire. When you asked him how he was, he would actually greet you with "X days, X months and X years until I'm out of here." He was, in fact, a mediocre to poor professor most of his career, but he had tenure, so he stayed to the end.

Consider this: who is more loyal? Would you consider the person who works at the same company for 20 years, but is a constant problem employee, never agrees with the mission, does as little work as possible and constantly talks badly about the company as being loyal? Or is the loyal one the person who believes in the company mission, gives 100% commitment, exceeds expectations in his or her work, and helps others succeed, but decides to stay only five years?

Loyalty to people is also one of my core values. The most difficult decisions I had to make as a leader were when I had to choose between my loyalty to a person and my loyalty to the organization and its mission. It often caused me to drag my feet in deciding to move someone out, even when I knew it was the best thing for the organization. In hindsight, I can say that most of those to whom I was too loyal ended up causing harm to the organization. Once I knew the right decision, I should have acted earlier. You must decide where your loyalty lies.

What do you see as character issues? What are those issues where you will draw the line and never cross it?

CHARACTERISTICS SHOULD BE A CONSCIOUS CHOICE.

Excellence is not often seen as a value, but for me, striving for excellence is important. Another way to put it is, "If it's worth doing, it's worth doing right."

I heard this from my father, my best teachers, and my Bible: "Do all things to the glory of God." There are always constraints of time, resources, knowledge, and other issues, but striving for excellence every time means you do your absolute best with what is around you.

Humility. True humility is not a false, self-effacing, humble pie thing. It's knowing what your true capabilities are, being grateful for them, and using them in a way that helps others. It is letting your actions and your impact speak for you.

Michael Jordan is an amazing athlete and I've always considered him one of the humblest superstars ever, not because of what he said or did off the court, but because of what he did on it. If he thought he had the best shot and was confident he could make it, he took the shot. If he thought someone else would have a better shot, he passed the ball and had them take the shot. Every year of his career, he was one of the leaders in scoring *and* assists. He was confident but humble. His actions didn't say, "Oh gee, I'm not such a great shot, you guys take the shot," and his actions didn't say, "I'm so great a shot, I am going to take every shot I can because I know I'm always better than you guys."

Tom Coughlin, who retired as president of Walmart USA and who also served as the Chairman of Enactus, often told the story about the day he was to interview for his first job at Walmart. He got to the headquarters early to prepare mentally for the big interview. As he sat in the parking lot, a guy drove up in a pickup and got out wearing khaki clothes. This guy started picking up the litter and paper that had blown into the parking lot that day. My friend thought, "What a conscientious custodian, arriving an hour before the office opens to make sure the parking lot is clean." At the appointed time, my friend went inside for his interview. When escorted to Mr. Walton's office, he was surprised to see that the khaki-dressed custodian sitting behind Mr. Walton's desk was actually Mr. Walton himself. Tom decided to join Walmart right then, before any questions were asked. Sam Walton, the founder of Walmart, was confident but humble. He always gave credit to his associates for the success of the company.

How you handle a crisis is a test of what you are made of. I have a friend who says you know what's in a glass when you shake it up and see what spills out. It's the same with people. When you're shaken up, how do you react? How do you speak, how do you treat others, how do you respect others? All are signs of the real you. Do you run and hide, freak out, yell a lot, or shift the blame to others? Or do you find real solutions to solve the crisis? Are you like the fighter pilot – calm and steady?

Punctuality. When I am late for a meeting, I have two standard lines: "My apologies. I do not like being introduced as the late Alvin Rohrs," or "My apologies. My goal is to never be late to anything but my funeral." I want to respect others' time and have them respect mine. To me, punctuality is not an issue of character. It's not immoral or unethical to be late, but I want people to know they can rely on me to be on time.

It was interesting to watch the last meeting I attended of the chairmen of the boards for all of the countries in Enactus. The Chairman from Germany said, "In Germany, if you are on time, you are late." Not many of the chairs from other countries shared his view of punctuality. Different cultures have different views. I have learned in the world of international business that while punctuality at business events is expected, it is not so much for social events.

Take on the new and the difficult. "Can't Never Could." Don't give up before you even try, just because you don't think you can do a task or because it looks too difficult. Be the person who steps up and gives it a try, no matter how tough it looks.

My good friend Robert Plaster was a very successful entrepreneur who built a large propane distribution company. He grew up in the Ozarks. His father died when he was 15, in the middle of the Great Depression. His mother worked hard to support her children and Bob went to work early in life to do his part. Whenever Bob said he couldn't do something because it was too hard, his mother always responded with, "Can't never could. Don't tell me you can't do something until you've given it your best effort. You haven't truly failed until you give up trying." This became Bob's theme: to try what others backed away from. He became known as the person who would do the hard work and the person to whom you gave the most difficult tasks. He was the person everyone counted on when the going got tough. He would stick with a task until it was finished.

Humor. On a bad travel day, I was standing in a very long line, waiting to report my lost luggage from a delayed flight. As we slowly moved forward, the man in front of me worked himself into a frenzy. When it was his turn, he began shouting and cursing at the woman behind the counter. After 15 minutes of being berated, the woman slammed her ink pen on the countertop and said, "Mister, there are only two people in the world who give a damn about where your luggage is, and one of us is losing interest very fast."

The rest of us in line cracked up and the guy cooled off. When it was my turn, I told the woman a joke my kids had told me the day before. This time she cracked up and thanked me for brightening her day. When my luggage finally arrived at my hotel, it had a "special delivery" tag on it. Several months later I was back in that line. When it was my turn, she broke into a big smile and retold me my joke because she remembered me. I decided then that I wanted to be that guy who brightened people's days by making them smile and laugh in tough situations. Humor is not a character issue, but it is part of my reputation.

Have you ever walked past a college classroom and heard economics students belly laughing? They do at Harding University. Dr. Don Difine has been the faculty advisor for Enactus at Harding for over 40 years. He incorporates humor in his approach to teaching economics. That is a rare talent.

Courage. I'm not sure if courage is something you seek or choose, or if it just shows up when it is required. When faced with a situation that requires courage, exercising it is a choice. One of the most courageous people I have worked with is Fatma Serry. She is the founding Country Leader of Enactus Egypt. When she started this work, she was not aware that her country would go through multiple political revolutions. She didn't know she would spend many nights sleeping in her office because of the Tahrir Square protests or other violence in the streets. But through years of turmoil in her country, she has built a successful organization. In most years, she raised more money than many of her peers in other, much more developed countries. Egypt won the Enactus World Cup three times, tied only with the United States for most wins. In her words, she was just doing her job, but the rest of us knew that it was her courage and passion which allowed her to prevail and to succeed in such challenging times.

Faith. For me, my Christian faith has been what has defined my character provided me peace during the storms and strength in the times of weakness. The Christian Bible has been my guide, and Jesus Christ has been my example and standard. This is an impossible standard, but, coupled with grace, mercy, and forgiveness, it has become my way of life: my ultimate journey. Faith is a very personal choice. It's your choice if you want to be known as a person of faith.

HOW WILL OTHERS SEE YOUR CHARACTER AND WHAT ARE THE CHARACTERISTICS YOU WANT TO BE KNOWN FOR?

What characteristics will you be known for? **You cannot control how others will behave or react to you, but you can control how you treat and react to others**. "Respected," "liked," "loved," "valued," "trusted," "feared," "hated by everybody but still got the job done," "always a winner no matter what it took." What are the words you want to be used to describe your legacy?

SUMMARY:

- Define your core values. They include character and characteristics that make up your reputation.
- Character is in your control.
- How you treat others will be a big part of your legacy.

ACTION STEPS:

- Create a list of your own core values. What do you want to be known for?
- Brainstorm how you will implement those values in your life and work.

CHAPTER FOUR

PROTECT THOSE CORE VALUES.

I was on a pheasant hunt with my good friends Jack and Troy Link, father and son. I felt like I was freezing to death. We were in South Dakota and it was my first pheasant hunt. We had gathered a large group of friends and colleagues for this event. The invitations went out in August when it was summer. At the time of the event in December, three feet of snow had fallen and the temperature flirted with zero, with a 15 M.P.H. wind. My immediate thought when I arrived: *They call this fun?*

The first morning I was a blocker, standing at the end of a half-mile-long field while other hunters were in the field walking towards me. Standing in the wind with no action, I got very cold and felt like an ice cube. As the birds approached, I was able to practice shooting, but I had gotten so cold and was such a bad shot, that the birds flew right past me. That burst of excitement and a drink of coffee warmed me up enough to get onto the old school bus that was being used to move hunters from one field to the next. I thought I was wearing good gloves and good boots, but my hands and feet were freezing.

I asked Jack Link if he had any better gloves I could borrow. He said, "Your gloves and boots are fine. But you've got it all wrong. Your hands and feet aren't cold because of poor gloves and boots. They're cold because you're not properly protecting your core. If you don't have enough clothing to keep vital organs – heart, lungs, liver, etc. warm, your body draws blood from your extremities to heat up your core. That blood flows away from your extremities and makes your feet and hands cold to save your core and save your life. If you want to keep your hands and feet from freezing, then add layers over your abdomen. Keep your coat zipped tight and add a vest or two." So, I added layers to protect my core and it made all the difference between a great experience and a miserable day. However, my shooting was so bad that the other hunters accused me of being a spy for PETA.

This experience gave me insight into my own life and work. Upon reflection, it made me realize that protecting our core values is what keeps us alive, but the extremities seem to get all the attention. **In your life and your work, protect your core values and the rest will be okay.**

PROTECT YOUR CORE VALUES BY CREATING RULES OF ENGAGEMENT.

Jack Shewmaker often told the story of bird hunting with Sam Walton and President Jimmy Carter in South Texas.

You can imagine all the added challenges of hunting with a former President of the United States and his cadre of Secret Service agents, gatekeepers, and support staff. It made the hunt even more challenging.

Mr. Walton's favorite dog was Ol' Roy. Walter Shields was Ol' Roy's trainer and handler, as well as Mr. Walton's ranch manager. As the hunt progressed, Ol' Roy and the other bird dogs were staring down a covey of quail in a big mesquite bush. The quail wouldn't move so Walter went in to flush the birds. Instead of birds flushing, a very big rattlesnake flushed and went straight for Ol' Roy and President Carter. Out of instinct, Walter jumped on the snake and landed with one boot on its head and one on its tail, trapping it to the ground.

This also resulted in the Secret Service agents pulling out their handguns and machine guns which were now all pointed at the snake and at Walter. As Jack described it, it was like one of those movie scenes where all the guns were out, and one wrong move would result in a bad shootout. Walter asked Mr. Walton, "What do I do?"

"Let me think on it," was the reply. If Walter took his foot off the head, he got bit. If he took his boot off the tail, it would wrap around his leg and eventually he would get bitten. "Walter," Sam said, "I'm going to aim my gun at the snake and count to three. When I get to three, you jump as high and as far away from me and the snake as you can, and I will shoot the snake."

By now the Secret Service agents had moved President Carter and themselves far from danger. Sam counted to three. Walter jumped. Sam shot. The snake died. After everything settled down, President Carter asked Walter,

"What were you thinking while you were standing on that snake?" In his slow Texas drawl Walter replied, "You know, Mr. President, you just don't do your best thinking when you're standing on a rattlesnake."

Don't wait until you're standing on the rattlesnake in the heat of the moment, when the pressure is on to decide how you will handle issues that challenge your core values.

Decide now what integrity means to you. Think through those scenarios that might challenge your integrity. Decide where you will draw the line before you come close to the line. Write them down and burn them into your brain so that when challenges come, you can protect your core values.

I remember my first business trip to Chicago. It was years ago when taxis only took cash. Every time I used a taxi and asked for a receipt, they gave me a blank one. When I got home at the end of the week, I tried to sort out which blank receipt went with which stop on my trip. I got them very confused, and it cost me a trip to the CFO's office to straighten this out.

I decided then that I would make each cabbie fill out the form, sign it, and date it. If they refused, I made sure I filled it in on the spot or as soon as possible and noted that I was the one who filled it out. It might seem like a minor thing, but it disciplined me to keep all my travel and expense reports accurate so that there would never be any question about my integrity on expense reports.

We all know people who have made serious career and personal mistakes because they got too drunk. The office holiday party, the summer picnic, or dinner at the boss' house, where a few too many drinks caused them to say things they shouldn't have said or to do things that made others doubt their judgement, even when they were sober.

I was at a trade event sitting alone at a table, when an old friend sat down beside me. We had both just heard President George W. Bush speak at this event. "What did you think of Bush?" he asked.

"I really enjoyed it. Especially his honesty about his personal failures early in life," I replied.

My friend continued, "After all the years you've known me and the many years we've been to this event, do you think I am as far in my career as you thought I'd be when we first met?"

I had to be honest, "Not really. I thought you'd be a CEO by now, or even earlier."

"Me, too," he said. "Listening to President Bush talk about his problem with drinking, I've just realized what damage drinking too much has caused my career. I never did anything crazy or stupid, but I always had to close the bar at every event and I had to be the life of the party. I showed up late for meetings because of that party the night before. I realize now that slowly, year by year, the problem got worse, and it caused people to lose their trust in me and my judgment. My career didn't die in a big drunken explosion; it died from a slow drowning."

My response was, "I'm sorry this has happened. Can you turn it around?"

"I'm not sure," he replied.

I asked, "Why did you decide to share this with me today?"

"Simple," he replied, "In all these years and at all these events, you're the one guy who I've never seen even tipsy and you are the only one who has refused to get me a drink when you know I've had too many."

He now controls his drinking, and he is now a CEO.

Set the rules of engagement for all of your core values before you are standing on the snake. Draw the lines that you will never cross.

You can push on the guardrails of your core values as you run the race of your life and career, bouncing from the left one to the right one, constantly challenging them to see how far you can push them before they break, or before you crash. But why? It's a waste of energy. Rubbing on the guardrails slows you down. Stay firmly between the guardrails and drive right up the middle of your core values so that you can accelerate even more.

Determine which words describe character issues you want to control and which characteristics you want to be known for.

SUMMARY:

↷ Protect your core values by creating rules of engagement. Don't wait until you are standing on the rattlesnake to decide how you will handle issues that challenge your core values.

ACTION STEP:

⇪ Determine what proactive practices you can do to protect your character and legacy before the heat is on.

CHAPTER FIVE

WHAT WILL YOUR IMPACT BE? HOW WILL YOU LEAVE THE WORLD BETTER THAN YOU FOUND IT?

"You've gotta tell the squirrel story!"

I hear that often. It's a story I like to tell that explains the abundance concept. It's a true story that unfolded when I was sitting in the woods, up in a tree seat, watching nature.

To my left, I heard a horrible racket and watched 50 yards away as a squirrel climbed up an oak tree and shook the branches to knock down a few acorns. He then scurried down the tree to grab them. As he was descending the tree, birds swooped in and stole his acorns, as did a deer and a raccoon. The squirrel chattered at them, scolding them, but by the time the squirrel got to the bottom of the tree, the acorns were all gone, except maybe one or two. He then went back up the tree and repeated the process for about 30 minutes. Then I noticed to my right another racket. It was another squirrel, but this one took a different approach. He climbed an oak tree and shook and shook and shook the branches, making it rain acorns. As the squirrel climbed down the tree, the birds swooped in, the deer arrived, and so did the raccoon. But the squirrel had dropped so many acorns that the other animals got all they wanted and there were plenty left for the squirrel to eat and to bury in the ground for the winter.

The first squirrel only did enough to take care of itself and, in the end, didn't even accomplish that sufficiently. The second squirrel created an abundance of acorns and had more than it needed and also provided food for its neighbors.

ACCELERATOR LEADERS CREATE AN ABUNDANCE TO DELIVER IMPACT.

Accelerator Leaders create an abundance. They produce more than they need in order to share with others. They know that helping others creates an abundance that helps us all. How you use your abundance to improve the lives of others is how you create impact. What impact is your abundance having?

Sam Walton, Jack Shewmaker, Robert Plaster and other entrepreneurs and business leaders create jobs, products, and services that improve our lives and provide money for great philanthropy. My friend, Dr. Johnathon Sears, is an eye surgeon who has saved many people from becoming blind. He is currently doing research that could eliminate most blindness in newborn babies. He is creating an abundance of sight. Doctors like him, and others in the medical profession, strive to improve health and save lives.

I was very fortunate to have exceptional educators who taught me well. My high school teacher, W. H. Hood, and Dr. Ed Clark, faculty advisor for the Southwest Baptist University Students in Free Enterprise team of which I was a member, were educators who shared an abundance of knowledge with hundreds of students. Educators such as these men create new knowledge and increase the knowledge of others, helping them to live lives of abundance. My friends Renee and Jeff Waters both have PhDs in music and create an abundance of joy and happiness—when they perform and through the creation of new music they compose.

What kind of abundance will you bring to the world? How much will your abundance impact others? How many others will you lift?

THE RIPPLE EFFECT DETERMINES HOW FAR YOUR IMPACT WILL TRAVEL.

The impact you make will be unique. It can be defined in broad, general terms here, since the rest of your life journey will sharpen the definition.

Think about your impact as a ripple in the water. Your most immediate impact is to your family and close friends. Then it expands to those with whom you work or go to school, then on to their connections, then to your employees or colleagues and, finally, to your customers or clients.

When I was a student participant in Enactus, I worked on projects that directly helped people. Then I became a faculty advisor who helped many students do many projects. Then I became a country leader who empowered hundreds of faculty advisors to empower thousands of students. That led to becoming the global leader, empowering country leaders who empowered thousands of faculty advisors and hundreds of thousands of students which, in the end, impacted millions of people.

Sometimes the further your ripple goes the less impact you can have in different parts of the ripple. As my ripple of impact expanded, my direct impact on some people declined, while it increased with others. As a student, I had deep connections to the people served by my project, which I gave up when I became a faculty advisor. But being a faculty advisor gave me deep connections to my students. I then had to give up that deep connection to students to become a country leader. Becoming the global leader meant I had to forego direct relationships with all the faculty. As my ripple of impact expanded, my direct impact on some people declined while it increased with others. It is a path my career took me down, and it required choices along the way about how much impact I could have, with whom and where.

You need to consider your calling. You might choose to seek global impact, or you might choose to focus predominantly on your family or your local community. The world needs people who build strong local communities and small businesses as well as those who build large companies and organizations that have a global impact. Personally, I started with a local vision that became national and then, over time, became global. However, through all the changes, I stayed true to my original vision: I wanted to help people live better lives through free enterprise by empowering them to maximize their potentials through free market economies, entrepreneurship, and business.

Dave Bernauer, a retired chairman and CEO of Walgreen's, told me that he and one of his best friends had the original goal after pharmacy school to own their own drugstore. Dave went to work at Walgreen's to learn what he could to prepare to open his own store. He liked working there and developing people there, so he stayed and climbed the ladder, eventually retiring as chairman. His friend opened his own drugstore and ran it his whole career until he, too, retired. They're still good friends. Whenever they get together, they compare careers and find that each is a bit envious at times of how the other one lived his career, but neither would have traded paths with the other. Dave Bernauer chose to join a large organization, creating ripples that went nationwide. His friend chose to own a local business and kept his ripples in one area, but that allowed them to go deeper.

What kind of impact do you want to have? How far will your ripples go? How will you multiply your impact to create abundance?

SUMMARY:

- Accelerator Leaders produce more than they need to share with others. They know that helping others creates an abundance that helps us all.
- Consider your calling: What do you want the depth and range of your impact to be?

ACTION STEPS:

- Define the impact you want to have and who you wish to benefit.
- Define the depth and range of your impact. How far will it reach?

CHAPTER SIX

―――――――――――――――――――

WHO WILL BE THERE TO CELEBRATE ON THE MOUNTAINTOP OR AT THE FINISH LINE?

So, there I was, swimming in Cleveland, in October. Outside. Not in a swimming pool or even a lake. I was swimming in a retention pool. You know, the kind that sits at the end of a big parking lot and collects all the runoff from the rains so as not to flood the storm drain system. This is not a spring-fed lake or water that has been through a filter. It was full of parking lot grime, winter salt, and sludge that had been building up for months, if not years. I was not alone in this swim. Dozens of other people were swimming as well, and most of them were much faster than me. Since I was not the lead dog, my view was rather ugly. All the fast swimmers had churned up the water and the sludge at the bottom. The water was now a murky brown, becoming black, and stuff was sticking to my swimsuit and my body, but I was loving it! How crazy is that?

This was no ordinary swim or college hazing. This was the Duck Days swim challenge organized by Manco, the makers of Duck Brand Duct Tape. My friend, mentor, and chairman of my board, Jack Kahl, had honored me by asking me to swim in the Duck Challenge. This had become an annual event that Jack and his team arranged to honor their annual success. It was patterned after the famous hula dance challenge designed by Sam Walton. He told his team that if their profits hit a record number, he would do a hula dance in a grass skirt on Wall Street. They hit the number, and Sam Walton did the dance.

Years earlier, Jack Kahl challenged his people that if they hit what appeared to be an unreachable sales number, he would swim across the duck pond – the dirty, stinky duck pond. They hit the number, and Jack swam the pond. The next year he set another unreachable number and they hit it. But this time his team wanted to join in the swim. The next year, it was suppliers who helped them hit the number, and they wanted to swim. The next year some of their retail customers even jumped in. Jack Kahl was the Enactus chairman and Manco was one of our largest donors, so when he asked me to join the swim, it was an honor, sludge and all.

Why would a rather large group of normally sane business people jump in a drainage pond in October in Cleveland? Because we wanted to be there when Jack Kahl and his family crossed the finish line. We wanted to be there when they were at the top of the mountain celebrating that year's victory. We did it out of respect, honor, and friendship.

Who will swim the pond with you? Who will be there when you cross your next finish line or are standing on top of the mountain you just climbed? If the answer is no one, I can assure you it will be lonely at the top. Crossing the finish line alone is a very hollow victory.

BUILD QUALITY RELATIONSHIPS.

My uncle in Texas called to tell me his granddaughter-in-law was in the hospital in India and asked for our prayers. She and her husband were on a trip there, and as they arrived at the airport to return to Texas, she became very ill. Adding to everyone's concern was that she was pregnant. Mother and baby were both at serious risk. I said a prayer, and then I contacted two of my best friends in India, Farhan and Shmita. Farhan assured me that the hospital my relative was in was one of the best in India and had a world class medical staff. Shmita informed me that her uncle was part of that world class medical staff, serving as a doctor and surgeon.

Shmita's uncle told her he would check on my Texas relative and send regular reports. It was a great comfort to me and to my family to know from trusted friends that the medical care she received would be top-notch. It was also very reassuring that a friend's family member was willing to personally check on her and send us reports. When my uncle called, he had no idea I had friends in India. When I called my friends, I had no idea how much they would personally help my family. It took several weeks, but mother (and soon baby) were ready to come home. They are doing well to this day. Had I not cherished and protected my relationships with Farhan Pettiwala and Shmita Ramkumar, and had I not asked for their help, the outcome might have been very different. I know the worry and fear of my family would have been much, much greater.

Quality relationships are one of your most important assets. **Quality relationships go beyond knowing people, having connections, networking, or liking on social media. Quality relationships are built with time and mutual respect.** If you make them one-way streets— "What do I get from them?" or "I'll call them when I need them"—it's not quality.

"I'll be there for you and I know you'll be there for me," is a quality relationship. To stay in balance, you need quality relationships in your family, social life, and career. These quality relationships can be your greatest support. If you are grounded in these relationships, and they're built on trust, then you have the foundation and the internal structure to be able to handle the challenges that come your way. Strong relationships are like rocks in the waves. They are the things you cling to when all else is shifting. At times there will be misunderstandings and confusion with those with whom you have quality relationships, but because of the strength of the relationship, those misunderstandings and confusion can easily be cleared up.

GROW CIRCLES OF TRUST… BUT ALSO LISTEN TO YOUR CRITICS.

Even though your relationships are quality, they will not all be equal. At different times in your life, you'll have varying amounts of time to devote to each relationship. Because of the nature of the people in the relationship, you'll also have a different level of trust with each of them.

You need to build circles of trust within each part of your life; some of these will intersect. The members of the most inner circle are those you trust the most, the ones you know you can share anything with, and they will never disclose that information to others without your permission. Those are the people you can trust with your fears, joys, future plans, and deepest secrets.

The next circle includes those you can trust, but you don't feel totally comfortable telling them everything. A person's position in your circles of trust is based on your trust level in that part of your life and how that person treats your trust. People will move back and forth between different levels of trust, depending on how close your relationship is or how they've handled your trust in the past.

I share everything with my wife, Elizabeth, in all parts of my life. My children are in the next circle, and then the rest of my family. The following circle of trust includes my closest, longtime friends. At the top of that list would be Thane Kifer, who is a banker, a real estate developer, and entrepreneur. We met in college and went through law school together. We were so scared of flunking our first semester of law school that we moved out of our apartments into a hotel room and sequestered ourselves for the entire study week and finals weeks. It's the closest we came to a foxhole experience, and it made us close friends.

This circle of trust also includes the Pallbearers. This is the name we have given to ourselves as we know we will be each other's pallbearers. For over 25 years, every Saturday morning at seven o'clock, a group of guys has met at my church for an hour. There were many who came in and out of this group, but there are five who have stayed consistent all 25+ years. Ray Leininger is our retired pastor, an engineer by education who likes to do woodwork and metalwork and teaches English as a mission in Russia. Mike Lenz is a mechanic, keeping the service trucks of our local electric co-op running and trying to make money from his family farm. Lane Nutt is an optometrist, angler, master gardener, and sports trivia nut. Cleo Cunningham owns a trucking company that hauls grain; he also drives one of his trucks.

We meet with whoever is home on any particular Saturday. We solve all the world's problems (but no one else listens), share our news about family and friends, share our struggles from the past week and discuss what we anticipate they will be for the week ahead. What is shared in the group stays in the group. Over the years, we have watched children and grandchildren grow up, mourned the death of Ray's wife, Judy, and rejoiced a few years later in his marriage to his second wife, Mary. We share joy and heartache. It is a group that gives me comfort and keeps me humble. When we gather, title, income, and status disappear. We're just guys going through life together.

Creating a circle of trust in your work has challenges. It can be difficult to be totally open and transparent with your supervisor, peers, and subordinates, especially as these relationships change. I had the opportunity to have board members and board chairs who allowed me to be open with them about the challenges the organization was facing or that I was facing personally. They helped me determine the best path to letting others know about these challenges.

It's difficult to tell your boss about any doubts you might have about your own abilities. It is also difficult to do this with peers who may be competition for your next promotion. If you let your guard down, they might use it to beat you to that next level. Getting too close to those you supervise creates issues as well. You don't want to be seen as playing favorites. You must stay objective enough to give honest feedback. Twice, I had to fire one of my best friends. It was extremely painful for them and for me. In spite of these challenges, you need a circle of trust in your career. Build it carefully and use it properly. It's not your complaint box, your gossip group, or where you go to diss other people. If you make it a confidential, safe space to let everyone grow, it will be valued and used wisely by others . . . most of the time.

MENTORS, COACHES, AND GUIDES.

Mentor – an experienced and trusted advisor. Coach – an instructor or trainer. Guide – a person who shows the way to others. Out of your circles of trust will come your mentors, coaches, and guides. Mentors are those who went before you, who have already experienced what you will be going through and will help you follow where they have been. Coaches are those who walk along beside you as they help you discover your own abilities and find your own path. Guides are the experts and authorities in a specific situation who show you the best way to a specific goal – for example, how to catch a rainbow trout, or the best way to reach a specific destination ("This is the way to the top of Mount Everest.")

A mentor is more likely to say, "This is what I did; you should do it as well." A coach might say, "What are the options in this situation and how can I help you analyze them? You will decide which to choose." A guide would say, "I'm a proven expert on how you do this or how you get there, so follow my instructions."

You choose some of your mentors, coaches, and guides, and some choose you or are chosen for you. My mother and father were my first mentors. No choice on my part or theirs. Most of those who served as chairmen of the board of Enactus were mentors and/or coaches. While I had input on who would be named, they were always elected by the board. Similarly, I had many teachers in schools that I did not choose, but a few of them became mentors by mutual choice.

Whether they are mentors and coaches by choice, force, or providence, use them wisely and listen to them well. However, do not assume that 100% of their advice is right for you at the time. Distill their advice. Filter it through who you want to be, what impact you want to make, who you want to join in your celebration.

Two of my board members, who were also my closest mentors, got very mad at me at a board meeting. One of my leaders had made a very serious error in judgment— not related to integrity—that cost us money and loss of momentum. I accepted the blame because it had happened on my watch and I did not call out that person at the meeting. This made these two mentors angry, and after the meeting they both told me rather forcefully, "If we know who made the mistake, we call them out in front of everyone else. This makes it clear to that person and the others in the room that you won't tolerate these kinds of mistakes. Public reprimand is good for the entire organization." They were both my seniors and superiors, so I assumed they were right.

At the next meeting the same person made another mistake, but not on the same scale. This time, when the board asked whose fault this was, I called the person out. As I threw my colleague under the bus, I could see the look of approval on the faces of my two mentors, but I could also see the faces of my leadership team and saw a look of horror and dismay as they now felt that they, too, could be thrown under the bus. I decided this advice was not for me. I met with each of my mentors and told them my reasons for not taking their advice and asked them to not require me to do so at board meetings. I met with the person I threw under the bus and apologized. I then met with the full team and did the same. It took me almost a year and three board meetings, before my team fully trusted me based on my actions.

GUIDES HAVE A DIFFERENT ROLE.

I was fishing in Alaska's Katmai National Park on the American river with my friend John Kahl, son of Jack Kahl, and our guide, Tom Beatty from the Royal Wolf Lodge. John and I had a stupid good day of fishing. We caught arctic char and giant rainbow trout with almost every cast. It was so crazy that while I was sitting on a boulder in the river resting, my fly accidently dropped in the water and a giant rainbow grabbed it right under my nose. We each caught over 100 fish that day. The only downside to the day was this great big 800-pound brown bear that kept coming down the river, chasing us out and sitting in the best pools.

Tom decided to avoid this intrusion, and the bear's big teeth and claws. He thought we should move up the river. We climbed the brush-covered ridge above the river to get to a path that would allow us to walk around the spot in the river where the bear was hanging out. As the guide, Tom led the way on this narrow path through the tall, thick brush.

Abruptly Tom turned around, looked me in the eyes and said, "Turn around and walk off the path quickly, but don't run."

Instead of obeying immediately, I stopped and asked him, "Why?" as he walked past me.

Then I saw an even bigger brown bear, whose head looked to be three feet wide, coming up the trail. He was only 10 yards away from me. Only then did I walk quickly off the trail, not running, but walking faster than I ever had in my life. After the danger was gone, Tom grabbed me by my shirt collar, looked me in the eyes, nose to nose, and said, "The next time I give you orders, you will obey them immediately. No questions asked, or you may die. Do you get it?"

"Yes, I do," I immediately replied.

When you use a guide for a specific purpose or to reach a very specific destination, pick the best guide who is truly an expert, the one who knows THE best answer. Then you must listen to the guide and do what he or she says. I have guided my friends fishing at places I've fished often, with great success. Nothing frustrates me more than when my friends decide they know better than I do and fish my location their way, using lures I would never use. When they catch no fish, they blame me for being a lousy guide.

Get the best guide. Get the best advice. Follow the best advice from the best guide. Get the best results.

There are some in your circle who play the role of mentor, coach, or guide at different times. You need to understand their role at that time and react accordingly.

DON'T IGNORE YOUR CRITICS.

While most of your critics will not be in any of your circles of trust, do not ignore them. Listen to them. They have a perspective you need to hear, and it may be a perspective that others share. Their perspective might even be right. You need to know this.

If those in your circle of trust do not criticize you from time to time, they are likely not as trustworthy as you think. Face it; you're not perfect. Don't you want your friends and family to tell you the truth instead of hearing it from some outsider or even an enemy?

Two of my dearest friends and closest mentors, who were also my biggest critics, were Jack Shewmaker and

Robert Plaster. Bob would call me and ask if I could go ride around the ranch with him. He had a beautiful ranch in the Ozarks with miles of spring-fed river running through it, surrounded by beautiful limestone bluffs. I'd go over and climb in his four-wheel-drive truck and we would ride around for a few hours. We would start by talking about various topics, while watching the deer and turkey and listening to the harmony of the river ripples. Then he'd stop the truck, look me in the eye, and tell me what I was doing that he didn't agree with. We would discuss it for a long time. Sometimes I'd persuade him to my side, but generally he was right. Because he was so direct, I knew exactly what he was thinking. Thankfully, he always criticized me in private, never in public.

Jack Shewmaker would also call me to meet privately; to grab lunch or to meet at his office, and we would do the same. However, if I brought something to the Board that I hadn't discussed with him in advance and he disagreed with it, he would very vocally criticize me in public. Needless to say, I learned to talk to Jack well before bringing anything to a board meeting. Even if we still disagreed on what was best for the organization, at least I knew what his objections were and that he would make them known rather forcefully at the meeting. It's much better to get hit by fire when you've had time to get your fire suit on.

My circle of trust, my mentors, coaches and guides, have changed over time. My father, W. H. Hood, Jim Sells, Bob Plaster, and Jack Shewmaker have all passed away. Others have changed interest and careers and we've lost touch, while new ones have been added. Having circles of trust in various parts of my life, work, spiritual, and social arenas has given me grounding and support. It's not about people pleasing; rather, it is about gaining the respect and trust of those you respect and trust. Through this effort, there are lots of upsides, but there is also one downside.

The only risk to trust is being betrayed. All betrayal begins with trust. My wife is a judge who handles divorce cases. Too often these cases involve good people who are on their worst behavior. At one time they loved each other madly, and now they're just mad. At the core of this love-turned-to-hate, there is usually betrayal. The deeper the love and trust was, the deeper the cut feels.

Betrayal and the power of forgiveness.

I have never been betrayed where the deepest cuts occur, by my wife or family. I have been betrayed by team-mates at work, friends, coaches, mentors, and guides, including some who were in my trusted circle.

Jesus teaches us through his life and words that we are to forgive those who betray us, whether or not they repent or apologize. This has been one of the hardest things for me to do in my faith walk. Even when I think I have forgiven someone, my rage can rise up out of the blue and I have to forgive again. That anger and hate only hurts me.

If you trust others, you will run a high risk of one or more of them betraying you. Even so, trust is worth the risk and the pain, just like love.

John Playter was a strong, but quiet, leader in our little town of Bolivar, Missouri. He was a pillar of the community and known for his integrity. Many of us knew that he was a Veteran of World War II, but we knew little of his service. He never spoke about it. Our pastor at church was preaching a series of sermons on forgiveness which were weighing heavily on John. One Sunday after the sermon, John went forward to the front of the church and began to read a statement. It was unlike John to command the floor, so we all listened intently, knowing these would be valuable words.

John shared his story from World War II. He had been stationed in the Philippines when the Americans surrendered to the Japanese and he became a prisoner of war. He was treated horribly and inhumanely by his captors. He was beaten and starved and required to do grueling manual labor. He was in the Bataan Death March and was on the Japanese ship the Shinyo Maru, also known as the "Hell Ship." It was torpedoed by American planes who did not know there were American troops on board. Of the 750 Americans on board, John was one of only 82 survivors. John saw hundreds of men drown and others get eaten by sharks.

He survived all of this and escaped to a beach in the Philippines, where locals hid him and cared for him until he was rescued by American troops. As we listened to this story of horror, there wasn't a dry eye in the house. John continued by saying that ever since then, he had hated the Japanese people with a passion. We all understood why. Then he said, "This hatred has eaten at my soul for my entire life. It has done me no good. Today I forgive my captors and I forgive all the Japanese people. I realize Jesus' command to forgive requires me to stop hating and forgive. Please think about those in your life you need to forgive. If I can forgive the Japanese, can't you forgive others for whatever it is they have done to you?"

For months, the people of our church and the whole community had a season of massive forgiveness. We saw families and friendships restored. Some were offered forgiveness but refused to accept or acknowledge it. It became clear that the person extending forgiveness became free from the weight and emerged with a renewed spirit, even if there was no reciprocity. John went on to tell his story at other places and was then convinced by good friends to record his life in his book *Survivor*. John has now gone to heaven, but is remembered by many as one the great men from the greatest generation. The local Rotary Club built a beautiful park and named it John Playter Park in his memory. When I am struggling to forgive someone who has wronged me, I go to Playter Park and sit in the gazebo. I remember John's story, and I find that, compared to his life, the wrong done to me was very small. If he could forgive, why not me?

I also remember my first trip to the Apartheid Museum in Johannesburg, South Africa. My son Ben was with me. It was a sobering and somber experience for him and for me. Ending apartheid was a big issue when I was his age. I was excited to help my son understand this part of history. When we approached the museum, I noticed giant pillars emblazoned with words I would naturally connect to a freedom exhibit, such as "Democracy" and "Freedom." There was one word that caught me by surprise: "Reconciliation." We went through the museum and saw the violence and atrocities of apartheid and the struggles following apartheid as South Africans formed a democracy. The word "Reconciliation" haunted me as we walked through these exhibits. I had been to many freedom shrines in America and other countries but had never seen the word "Reconciliation" in any of the displays.

When I got home, I reread *A Slow Walk to Freedom*, Nelson Mandela's autobiography. It was then that I fully understood why reconciliation was so prominent in the freedom of South Africa. When he was released from prison, Nelson Mandela had every reason, and arguably every right, to seek revenge and retribution against his captors and those who enforced apartheid. He knew that for the good of his own people and for the good of all of South Africa, that reconciliation, not retribution, was the true path to peace, democracy and eventual prosperity. He was heavily criticized and challenged for his stand, but he won, and South Africa won. Nelson Mandela realized and utilized the power of forgiveness. In 2015, the Enactus World Cup was held in Johannesburg and the all-country, all-staff dinner was held at the Apartheid Museum. It was a wonderful sight to see my friends and colleagues from 36 countries all learning about the power of forgiveness. At this event I had the privilege of meeting and getting to know Swati Mandela, Nelson and Winnie Mandela's granddaughter. She now refers to me as her friend, which I consider one of the highest honors I have received.

Another amazing example of forgiveness I witnessed was that of Serry Kone. Serry lived in Côte d'Ivoire, was separated from his family and sold to a cacao farmer as a child slave. He lived in horrible conditions and worked long hours at hard labor. One day he tried to help another boy slave with his work and was beaten mercilessly by the farmer. That night, Serry ran and ran until he found himself in the city. He found his way to an orphanage where he was eventually reunited with his family. Serry went to school and eventually earned his way into Brigham Young University–Hawaii.

He joined the Enactus team and told them of the conditions in his home country. The faculty and students followed his lead and developed an incredible program to improve life in one village in Côte d'Ivoire. They taught farmers how to use modern methods so that they would no longer use children for labor. The Enactus team helped build a school for the children, who now had time to go to school as they no longer worked from sunrise to sunset. The team also developed a micro-lending program to help women start and run their own businesses. They developed a machine to turn piles of discarded cacao husks into compost and fertilizer.

They even eliminated the scourge of malaria by drying up all of the water holes and building tanks to grow tilapia. The concept worked like this: mosquitoes landed on the water in the tanks to lay their eggs. Fish ate the mosquitoes and their eggs. This creative way to eliminate malaria also resulted in more protein in the villagers' diets and a new product to sell.

Serry and his Enactus team took this program from one village to the next and then the next until they reached the village where Serry had been enslaved and beaten. Serry and the students went to the farmer who had beaten him. Serry was no longer a little kid. He was now a full-grown, healthy man, much bigger and stronger than the aging farmer. There were no blows and no violence. Serry hugged him. Then he proceeded to show the farmer how to change his methods so that he would never again use child labor. Furthermore, the farmer improved his quality of life. Serry still carries the scars from his beating, but the scars on his body were never allowed to scar his soul.

The adage "Fool me once, shame on you; fool me twice, shame on me" seems to ring true with betrayal as well. **Give forgiveness and then reconciliation a try. If your offer of reconciliation is rejected, move on. If your offer is accepted, give it your best efforts.** Give enough trust to provide a valid test. If the relationship can be restored, it might become even stronger and better than before. If the test fails, you can move on, knowing you gave it your best. When I have handled betrayal well and offered reconciliation that didn't work, it still made a positive impression on those involved and even upon many who were just observers. It also freed me from the burden of anger.

SUMMARY:

- ⇗ Build quality relationships based on time and mutual respect.
- ⇗ Consider those in your life who play the roles of mentor, coach, or guide and react accordingly.
- ⇗ Listen to your critics.
- ⇗ Reconcile with and forgive those who may have hurt you in the past.

ACTION STEPS:

- ⚑ Create a diagram of your circles of trust and add the names of those in each ring of the circle.
- ⚑ Create a list of your past and current mentors, coaches, and guides by category. Determine which ones overlap.
- ⚑ Who are your critics? Analyze the criticism and see if it's valid.
- ⚑ Who do you need to reconcile with? Create a list.

CHAPTER SEVEN

DETERMINE YOUR STARTING POINT. WHAT ARE YOU TRULY CAPABLE OF?

Now that you've determined your end goal, it's time to identify your starting point. To do that, you must analyze and understand where you are now, who you are now, and what you're capable of achieving. It's time to put egos aside and take inventory.

WHAT ARE YOU CAPABLE OF ACHIEVING? NEVER UNDERESTIMATE YOUR ABILITIES.

Thanks to the generosity of my dear friend Jack Kahl, I've had the privilege of fishing the Super Bowl of rainbow fly fishing – Katmai National Park in Alaska. This good fortune also gave me the opportunity to fish the same waters with our mutual friend Jack Shewmaker, the former president of Walmart.

> One beautiful summer day, Jack Shewmaker and I set out to fish the lower end of the American River. We took a float plane to the river and then hopped in a small boat with a guide who took us way upstream to begin fishing our way down river. At times we fished from the boat and at other times we landed the boat and fished from the shore – all the while dodging giant Kodiak brown bears. They allowed us to cohabit in range, as long as we left them and their salmon alone.
>
> We had a wonderful day and really slayed the fish, catching rainbow, char, and grayling. How many, I don't know, because I don't count how many fish I catch. That's something I learned from Jack Shewmaker. He was a master fly fisherman. While I fished these great waters for one week every few years, he fished them for several weeks every year. His cast was so perfect, there were times I would just stop fishing and watch him. Brad Pitt's character in "A River Runs Through It" had nothing on Jack Shewmaker.
>
> If you asked Jack how many fish he caught a day, he would say, "I think I saw a fish." He'd learned that a good day of fishing wasn't about the number caught,

but the experience of catching them. His nickname at the lodge was "The Vacuum" because we all learned that if you fished behind Jack in the river there were no fish left by the time you arrived down river. Even if you fished in front of him and thought that you had caught every fish in the river, he would come right behind you and catch more. And his fish were often bigger than yours.

At the end of the day as we motored down the river to catch the float plane home our guide stopped the motor cold. The sudden force knocked Jack and I from our seats, and we hit the deck. "Is it a bear?" Jack asked. You didn't want to hit one of those monsters with a small boat.

"No," said the guide, "but it's a monster alright, a monster rainbow." Good guides have great instincts and a trained eye. Sure enough, across the river was a monster rainbow trout rising again and again to snatch bugs. We had already had a great day catching fish that would have been considered monsters back home. But this—this was an Alaskan monster, at least three times the size of a monster rainbow at home.

I asked if we had time. Jack and the guide laughed. "For that fish, we'll make time," they said in unison. I told Jack to go for it.

Jack replied, "I caught the last one, it's your turn." I knew this was just Jack's way of being gracious. The guide tied the boat to the bank, and I stood up and started casting. The other bank was 30 yards away, and the current in the middle of the river was running much faster than the current in front of us. I cast and cast and cast. My fly would land too far in front of the fish; the middle current would grab the line, jerk the fly away from the monster and whisk it down the river. Then I'd cast too close to the monster, it would spook and dive down into the water, and then we'd have to wait for it to feel safe and rise again. Thirty minutes passed, and my arm and shoulder ached from all the casting. "I give up," I said as frustration got the best of me. "I can't make that cast and my arm is too sore to try one more time."

Jack looked at me with surprise and said, "Wow! I've known you for over 20 years and have never heard Alvin Rohrs say, 'I quit,' or 'I can't do that.' There's something I know that you don't. I know you can make that cast. I've been watching you and you've made much harder and more challenging casts all day long. So, are you really going to quit?"

I was not about to let down my mentor, the godfather of my daughter Jaclyn, and the man who helped me turn my organization around. I stood up and grabbed my rod. Then Jack said, "Use the energy of the river, ignore the hazard, and forget how big the fish is." His words hit me right between the eyes. My arm and shoulder were tired because I had not been using good technique on this fish. A fly rod is a spring that stores and releases energy. I was using just my arm and shoulder to try to muscle the line across the river.

The proper technique is to use the energy of the river. You let your fly catch the surface of the water and let the current carry it downstream. You load your rod with that energy, and just as the rod is bending, you pop the fly off the surface and the rod springs back like a rocket. The line shoots through the rod and stretches way over your head and behind you. Then, just at the right split second, you pop the rod forward and the line races forward, bringing with it all the power you need to reach your spot. Instead of pumping my arm back and forth in broad motions, all I needed to do was move it methodically from 10 o'clock to 2 o'clock, just six inches both ways. The energy of the river would land the fly.

IGNORE THE HAZARD. DO WHAT YOU KNOW TO DO.

I had been so focused on the rapid current in the middle of the stream that I'd been over-compensating. Jack also reminded me that the size of the fish didn't matter; it was the cast that mattered. I was so focused on the monster that I didn't focus on my cast. When I relied on the energy of the river, my cast landed in exactly the right spot, a spot the size of a dinner plate three feet in front of the monster.

The fly floated slowly down the stream as I counted one, two, three, then WHAM! The monster hit it. I set the hook and the fight was on. The monster and I were now using the energy of the river to fight our battle. She would head into the strong current hoping to break the thin line and I would ever-so-gently respond, so as not to break the line, causing her to turn her head so that she was now sideways in the current, fighting the current instead of riding it. This seesaw battle went on for 30 minutes before she decided to surrender. I brought her to the boat and removed the hook. She was tired, but no worse for the fight. Fish don't have nerve endings in the lips and jaw, so they don't feel pain. They fight because of the tension. I held her gently in the water until she had enough new energy to dive to the bottom and find a good resting spot. As she was swimming off, the guide said, "Wait, we forgot to measure her." Simultaneously, Jack and I replied, "It doesn't matter." We both knew it was the size of the experience that mattered, not the size of the fish.

Had it not been for Jack, I might not have realized that I could do that. I'd made a thousand casts that prepared me for that cast.

Use the right technique; use the energy of the river; forget the hazard; forget the size of the challenge. You've got this! **It takes reflection and outside feedback to discover the real you.**

TOOLS FOR EVALUATION: THE MIRROR, THE SNAPSHOT AND THE VIDEOS.

To accelerate ourselves, we have to know ourselves, our abilities and our capabilities. What had happened during that fish fight was that I looked in the mirror, into my soul, and decided, *I'm not good enough to catch this fish and my arm can't go one more round.* When I considered just that moment in time, the snapshot view of the situation, I determined I couldn't do it. But when Jack considered the long view (the video of our experience together), he came to a different conclusion, one that reflected the accumulation of thousands of snapshots. The mirror, the snapshot and the video are tools that will enable you to truly understand your potential impact. Using just one does not give you an accurate picture. You need all three to discover what you are capable of achieving.

MIRROR, MIRROR ON THE WALL.

"When things are going great and you're winning, you should first look out the window and appreciate all those who helped you win. Then look in the mirror and congratulate yourself. When things are going badly, and you're not winning, you should first look in the mirror and take ownership of those factors that you can control. Then look out the window and see what outside factors or people are preventing the wins."

The first time I heard this was from Mr. Hood, my high school vocational agriculture teacher from Pleasant Hope High. He was my first non-parental mentor. Mr. Hood had a great reputation as a teacher and was the wise old owl to whom everyone listened. I was quite surprised and pleased to see one of the lessons I learned from him conveyed 20 years later in Jim Collins' book, *Good to Great,* as part of his description of a level-five leader. "Looking in the mirror, honest self-reflection, is the first step in developing good self-awareness."

It's a bit spooky to actually stare at yourself in the mirror, but it's a pretty good way to focus on yourself. This is true whether you do it by literally staring at yourself eye-to-eye, or by sitting in the woods, or in your favorite chair. Reflection requires quiet, calmness, and time. It involves being honest with yourself about who you are and what you can do, as well as answering why you're doing it in the manner that you've chosen.

I prefer the woods or sitting in a small boat on my pond. Maybe a garden or just an empty hotel room between meetings will work for you. Mirrors are the first step, but they only provide one point of data and one person's perspective. You must be careful not to distort or misapply the information.

A great example of distortion occurred during my first visit to Silver Dollar City, a theme park that celebrates life in the Ozarks in the 1800s. (They have some killer roller coasters.) My initial visit was as a child during the first week my family lived in Missouri. My dad's new boss wanted to show off our new home in the Ozarks. One of the attractions was a Hillbilly Fun House that used optical illusions like water running uphill and people in rooms that looked upside down. The hall of mirrors was designed to change how you looked. Some made you look taller, shorter, heavier, or thinner. These fun house mirrors really distorted how we saw ourselves.

I have since learned that mirror makers make mirrors that distort on purpose. Some stores use mirrors that make you look thinner, so you are more likely to buy the clothes you're trying on, or they maximize light reflection to make you feel happier. Our minds can distort the truth when we look into our own mirrors. We look at ourselves, but our mind performs its own version of Photoshop. If we aren't true to ourselves, we can distort our realities during our time of reflection. The only way we can see ourselves as others see us is to be truly honest with ourselves.

Another distortion trap to avoid when looking into the mirror is best illustrated by an incident that occurred at my office when a murder of crows invaded (a "murder" is what you call a flock of crows). There is a tree just outside my former office that is apparently the perfect spot for crows to hang out. My office has large, tinted windows, and at certain times of the day, they act as mirrors reflecting the crows in the tree. Crows are territorial and love the members of their own murder, but they don't want any other murders to invade their turf. So, when these crows look in the mirror, they see a second tree and a second murder, and they attack. They will hit the window over and over making a horrible racket until someone goes outside to chase them off or until the sun moves and the window no longer reflects the perceived threat. They have attacked the window so often and so hard that they have broken the weather seal.

As I was watching this assault one day, it occurred to me that in my last self-reflection session I had been beating myself up over something that was ancient history in my life. I kept attacking myself in the same way those crows were attacking their own reflections. If you are using your self-reflection time to beat yourself up, STOP.

TAKE A SNAPSHOT

My driver's license photo makes me look 10 years older and maybe a bit like a drug user. It was taken the day I arrived home from a two-week trip to Asia, when my sleep patterns were totally out of whack and I hadn't had good rest for days. That's my excuse, what's yours?

Don't you hate your driver's license photo? Mine wasn't taken at the best time, but it is an accurate picture of what I looked like at that time on that day and at that place. The truth is, I hate it because it's accurate. I hate it because when others see it, they see the truth of that moment. A valuable self-evaluation tool is to reflect on a snapshot of yourself in a particular time and setting. It's taking an authentic look at your condition at a moment of time that also allows truthful input from those around you. Having friends, coaches, and mentors who will give you honest feedback is critical to this strategy.

You can request direct feedback, but for those who find it difficult to offer brutally honest feedback, a number of quality 360-degree evaluation tools are available online from credible sources. This enables others to provide anonymous, truthful input. This process makes me uncomfortable, but it's valuable because outside input gives you additional data points to add to your self-reflection.

Snapshots can also be distorted if we alter the input in a way to make us look good. But if you ignore the input, the exercise is also a waste of everyone's time. After a 360-degree evaluation of one of my senior officers, I shared the results with her. I explained that her performance suffered because she was having difficulty getting along with her peers and that her subordinates were afraid of her. One subordinate even compared working for her to the scene in the movie *Schindler's List* where the commandant of the concentration camp would step onto the balcony of his office with a sniper rifle and randomly shoot a prisoner. "Her rage is so random we don't know when or how to react," one employee said.

Her response to my coaching was predictable. "I am who I am. I'm not going to change, so they need to figure out how to work with me." She was very self-aware, but really didn't care about how that affected her team or her performance. That attitude doesn't lead to accelerated leadership. Moving her out was an easy decision.

VIDEO REFLECTION

History matters. While snapshots help you reflect on one time and place, and mirrors allow us to self-reflect, videos serve as a collection of snapshots over time. Videos enable us to reflect on our entire life's journey with those who shared it. Not only had Jack Shewmaker watched me fish all that day, he'd watched me fish for years. More importantly, he had watched my life and career and had helped shape both of them.

On the river that day, he knew from his mental video that I was no quitter and that I had abilities I didn't recognize. In my career, he had the same long-term video view of my work. At times when I saw no answer, he helped me find one. When I saw barriers too high, he helped me see opportunities to scale them. For videos, you need friends and colleagues who have seen you in action over a longer period of time. Are we better than we once were, or worse? Have we been building skills and knowledge to be ready for that big new challenge? The video you've made with your friends, family, and colleagues can give you the answers. Spend time reviewing the scenes of your life's video with honesty. Invite feedback from those who know you best.

To find your starting point, use mirrors, snapshots, and videos for true self-assessment. Then you are ready to answer the "why," which will tell you what you are truly capable of.

DETERMINING THE WHY

"The person that knows 'how' will always have a job, but the person that knows 'why' will always be the boss."

These were the words I heard from my Vocational Agriculture teacher, Mr. Hood. They hit me right between the eyes, and I burned them into my brain. I thought they were brilliant and original. It wasn't until college that I read them in a book of quotes with no author attributed, but still I thought Mr. Hood was brilliant.

Later I learned that this message was, in fact, directed at me. After failing as a welder, electrician, carpenter, and mechanic, Mr. Hood told me bluntly, "Son, you're going to need to make your living with your brain because your hands just don't get it. You need to go to college to learn the why because you're no good at the how." For the record, while I did fail at shop class, I was elected president of my FFA chapter, and I was crowned the state champion chicken judge. If you want help selecting the best eggs and the best chicken to buy, I'm your man.

The moral of the story is that you need to answer three questions to find your starting point: *Why you?*, *Why here?*, and *Why now?*

On the farm where I grew up, one of my jobs was to be the shepherd. To non-shepherds, sheep all look alike. They see the flock, not the sheep. As has been said, "Every sheep knows his shepherd's voice, and every shepherd knows each of his sheep." At one point I had 100 sheep. I knew each one by name and by personality. While they are a herd animal by instinct, each one has a distinct personality, and a shepherd gets to know how to work with each one.

Since kindergarten we've all been told that every snowflake is different, and like snowflakes, each of us is unique. Science has backed this up. As the human genome has been unraveled, it tells us that indeed we are each different, and yet we're all linked.

There are 7 billion people on the earth. That's a big flock that looks pretty homogenous, but there are actually 7 billion unique individuals with distinct personalities, skills, and capabilities.

You're not just one in a million. You are, in fact, one in seven billion people. Own that. Believe that and live that.

WHY YOU?

My faith experience tells me that each one of us was created by God to make a unique contribution to serve God and his people. Your experience may tell you something else, but however you get to the conclusion, the fact remains that you are one unique person out of seven billion and you have a unique contribution to make to this world. Inventory what makes you unique. I was a state champion chicken judge—top that.

Your genetics, family and cultural environments, and life experiences have influenced who you are, where you are, and what you can accomplish. Use the virtual mirror, snapshots and videos to answer these whys and it will help you determine an honest starting point.

Genetics serve as a baseline. Unlike issues of character that are in your control, genetics are totally out of your control. They were set when you were born. Inventory the genetic markers that contribute to your uniqueness: tall, short, heavy frame, slender frame, skin color, hair color, and other features. Some of these can be altered, but for the most part, they are what they are. While you are similar to others in appearance, you are unique. Even identical twins aren't 100% identical. **Your genetic uniqueness is an asset, not a liability. Determine how your unique genetic characteristics can be utilized to accelerate your impact.**

Our family environment and culture also contribute to our uniqueness. Just look at the map of the USA and you can instantly see differences based on urban, rural, suburban, southern, northern, west-coast, or east-coast upbringings. Nature and nurture both affect our behavior and our eventual impact.

Whether influenced by genetics, nature, or nurture, the challenge for each of us is to identify how our unique genetics and family environment can be used to accelerate our impact. Don't get trapped in allowing genetic characteristics, which are out of your control, or environmental conditions, which are changeable, to form roadblocks to your acceleration.

Life experiences add to our uniqueness and blend with our genetics and environment to make us who we are. We have shared experiences, friends, and families that influence us, but each one of us has a unique set of experiences that shapes each life. School, sports, movies, jobs, relationships, and travel all shape who we are. Inventory those experiences that make you unique and evaluate how they can be an asset to accelerating your impact. What have you learned from them – good and bad? How have they shaped your view of the world, your relationships, your friends, and family? How have they shaped who you are now and the person you know you can become?

USE YOUR GENETICS, FAMILY ENVIRONMENT AND LIFE EXPERIENCES AS ASSETS TO ACCELERATE YOUR IMPACT. DON'T USE THEM AS EXCUSES TO UNDERACHIEVE.

Part of my life experience was living at boys' ranches. My parents, Wayne and Mona, worked at four different homes for boys. Throughout their careers they helped raise 1,500 boys who had previously been abused, neglected, or abandoned. Over 95% of the boys went on to live normal lives, which is an extraordinary accomplishment for children who had been written off by society. My parents' success was based on giving the boys unconditional love, a dose of structure and discipline, and teaching them the value of work. Every boy had a chore, a job they did for pay, and an opportunity to have his own farming business.

Every boy who came to live with them had to choose to live there and make a conscious choice to stay. One part of the onboarding process played out as my father would pull out a big file folder that contained a written record of the boy's life to that point. It included his family history and, in some cases, atrocities or records of crimes committed by him or against him. My father would say, "In this first file is everything that has happened to you and been done by you. This file will be closed and never referred to again. No other boy will know what is in it unless you lie to them and I have to set the record straight."

Then he would pull out a new clean file folder and hand it to the boy and say, "This is your new folder. It's empty. Whatever goes into it is totally up to you. You can fill it with bad things or good things, but if you choose to live with us, you start with a clean slate." These boys were my friends and playmates all my life. It was amazing to see how powerful a clean slate can be and how making good choices can overcome what others saw as bad genetics and unchangeable attitudes and trajectories.

HOW DO GENETICS, ENVIRONMENT AND LIFE EXPERIENCES HELP YOU ANSWER THE QUESTION, WHY HERE?

This question involves both your geographic location and your professional advancement. Usually, they are tied together. Whether you believe in providence, as I do, or coincidence, there are many things that have led to your current geography. I was born in Texas, lived in Montana, and moved to Missouri when I was eight. I now live 30 miles from where I grew up. Some would say I have gone nowhere, but from this home base I've travelled to all 50 States and 40 countries. Even if you are living in the house in which you grew up, your location still makes you unique. In fact, if you're living in the house you grew up in, you are uncommon in this day and age.

Consider all the circumstances that have put you where you are today. Are you living where you plan to stay, or do you intend to move on to another location? Either way, you're where you are for a reason and you should take full advantage of your location.

For those who are planting roots, the challenge is in not taking your location for granted. My friends in New York who tease me for living in what they call "fly-over" country always brag about the great city theatres, museums and restaurants. Then, when we compare notes, they often find out that I, this country boy, have been to more Broadway shows and museums than they have. When I visit the city, I take full advantage of my limited time. When you know your current location is temporary, whether for months or a few years, you must realize that you are where you are for a reason. Add value while you are there.

Consider the same for your career. Where are you in that journey? Whether you are a student or preparing for retirement, there have been many turns and twists to get you to where you are now. Consider how these have made you unique. Consider why you are sitting in the classroom or office or truck that represents your current career. You are in a geographical location and in a specific point in your career path. What will you do with it?

WHY NOW?

This is a unique and incredible time in your life and in human history. This is a wonderful time to be alive. The computing power you hold in your hand in your smart phone is greater than the computing power NASA used to put the first man on the moon. You can access all recorded human history and knowledge from anywhere on the planet in seconds. Over the past 15 years, extreme poverty has been cut in half around the world, and infant mortality has been reduced by 80%. The nations of the world have signed up for the Sustainable Development Goals that aim to end extreme poverty by 2030. We have the technology and brainpower to end extreme poverty, and medical science is finding cures for diseases and illnesses once thought incurable.

Consider where you are on your career-path spectrum from rookie to veteran. Evaluate the timing in your life and how your life fits into the timeline of human history. How does your uniqueness fit? Why now? Because it *is* now. Now is the time to accelerate your impact no matter where you are in your life and career cycle.

If you can answer the questions, *Why you? Why here?* and *Why now?* you can accurately determine what you are truly capable of achieving and identify a realistic starting point.

"Moxie" is an American slang word, which means determination or nerve, but when I think of moxie, I think of my Chinese friend Margaret Ranzman, Chairman and CEO of Dan Dee Manufacturing. If you ever bought a plush toy in a large retail store, the odds are about 60% that you bought one of Margaret's products.

When I met her she was already very successful. We were at dinner in Hong Kong at a rooftop restaurant overlooking the city. I just had to know her story.

Her family lived on the mainland and moved to Taiwan after the Communist revolution. In the transition, her family lost everything. Margaret went to school and studied business. She got several jobs and made some money, most of which she saved. When China first opened up manufacturing zones on the mainland, Margaret decided that this was her chance to make it big. She moved into a very small apartment, rented a small office and installed a phone line. She was confident she could manufacture and export something, but wasn't yet sure what that something was.

The phone rang. It was a surprise, because she had not yet listed her number anywhere. She answered. It was a wrong number. Before hanging up, the caller asked her if she made men's sweaters. "Let me put you on hold and check," she replied, even though there was no hold button on her phone. She held the receiver to her coat to shut off all sound and then rapidly reviewed her life. The snapshot of sitting in a room with nothing but a desk and phone told her she could not make sweaters. She looked in the mirror. She knew she had the skills, the grit and the commitment to do whatever she set her mind to. She already knew that she wanted to be a manufacturer and exporter, but she just didn't yet know of what. She then ran the video of her life through her mind.

When Margaret was a child, her family had moved to an entirely new place. They went from being highly successful to losing everything and starting over from scratch. She had learned how to be resourceful, how to marshal scarce resources to survive, and how to pick herself up if she failed. Compared to where she came from, making sweaters seemed rather simple. Looking around, she knew she had nothing to lose and up was the only direction she could go. In just a few seconds she made up her mind. "Yes, I can make men's sweaters. How many do you need and by when?" She replied. She got the order. Then she spent the next several weeks finding a manufacturer, suppliers, and an exporter. She delivered her first order early and under budget. She accelerated herself into becoming a textile manufacturer and eventually one of the largest manufacturers of plush toys. She never lost her moxie.

Now let's prepare to accelerate your unique impact.

SUMMARY:

- Avoid focusing on hazards or the size of the challenge you face. Focus on the best approach and reflect on valuable feedback to tackle the hurdle.
- It's the experience that counts.
- To find your starting point, use virtual mirrors, snapshots and videos for true self-assessment.
- You are a unique, one-in-seven-billion person. Use your genetics, family environment and life experiences as assets to accelerate your impact.

ACTION STEPS:

- 🖎 Use the answers to *Why you? Why here?* and *Why now?* to inventory what makes you unique.
- 🖎 Evaluate which unique features you perceive to be assets and those you perceive to be liabilities.
- 🖎 Use your list of liabilities and reevaluate them so that you may turn them into assets.

CHAPTER EIGHT

DON'T LET THE IMMEDIATE GET IN THE WAY OF THE IMPORTANT.

After one of our prospecting luncheons in Dallas, my chairman, Jack Shewmaker went, on to his business commitments that afternoon. I went on to visit other prospects. Coincidently, at the end of the day, we happened to be at the same gate at the airport. Jack was heading off to somewhere in South Texas, and I was heading off to Houston. Jack said, "Why don't you join me in South Texas to hunt quail; I think you'll enjoy it?" I thanked him but declined, saying that I had never hunted quail before. Besides, I had commitments in Houston and couldn't change my plans. In my mind, I was picturing myself looking like an idiot, missing the birds and getting laughed at. Jack said he understood and that we would catch up later. A few weeks later I got a handwritten note in the mail from the desk of

Jack Shewmaker that read: *Sam Walton and I had a great time hunting in Texas. Never let the immediate get in the way of the important.*

Jack made it very clear that I had just blown a major opportunity. Spending two days with Sam Walton, the founder of Walmart, was the dream of any fundraiser for any organization. A dream I had passed up. "Don't let the immediate get in the way of the important" was a lesson I learned that I tried to practice in my own career. Unfortunately, I had to relearn the lesson over and over. What Jack was really saying is, *focus on the important.* Don't let the immediate keep you so busy you can't do the important. You need to prioritize.

In this era of emails, texts, Snapchat, and whatever new social media comes along, there is an even greater sense of immediacy and urgency than when Jack Shewmaker sent me that note. It's extremely difficult in this era of instant gratification, instant news, and live streaming to keep your focus on the important. The immediate comes at us faster than an Indy race car or a jet; it now comes at the speed of light. The time we're allowed to react is very short. There was a time when you got a phone message and people didn't expect it to be answered for a day or two. You actually had time to read letters and write letters and time to react. Now everything moves at super speeds, and this increased pace requires focusing on what is important—your impact.

What is important is your legacy. You've envisioned what it is and assessed your own ability and potential. Make it come true. How do you keep your eye on this legacy while dealing with stuff coming at you at the speed of light?

KEEP FOCUSED AND LOOK FORWARD

I learned a great lesson on focus in Hawaii. My organization was holding an event in Hawaii for our students, faculty, and business partners there. We needed a keynote speaker who would attract a good crowd. One of the most popular local celebrities on the islands was a news anchor named Dan Cooke.

To my good fortune, Dan grew up in my hometown and I went to college with his brother. Dan was also a celebrity to us farm boys who saw him living the dream life on the beach in the sun. Dan agreed to speak, and he did draw a good crowd. He made us look good to our partners on the islands. I honestly didn't expect much of a keynote address. After all, he just read the news, right?

To my surprise, he was an excellent speaker. One of the things he told our students was about his first week in Hawaii. Everyone told him that he had to do the bike-down-the-volcano tour, which he did. You ride a bus to the peak and then ride a bike down the volcano. The guide told him to be very careful not to bump into the volcanic rock along the trail, as it was sharp and would cut him. Dan asked, "How do I avoid getting cut?"

The guide replied, "Focus on looking far ahead to where you want to go and do not look at the rocks right around you. If you look at the rocks on one side, you will steer away from them and hit the rocks on the other side. You'll crash and get cut. If you keep looking forward and focus on the light at the end of the trail, you will forget about the rocks. You will stay on the trail and you'll be safe." Wow! What great advice for our students and for me.

I was at a lodge on one of my outdoor adventures, and one of the other guests was bragging about what a great outdoorsman he was. He continued at length all through the first night's dinner, so much that we all knew he was a poser. The next morning at breakfast, he was trying to get his new expensive binoculars to work but he couldn't get anything into focus. He started swearing and threw them in the trash.

I asked if I could have them and he said yes. I put them in my backpack, but then felt a bit guilty, so I showed him how to make them work. It always annoys me when they show someone using binoculars in a movie or TV show. They show two circles the person is looking through to give you that person's view. This is bogus. Good use of binoculars means adjusting both tubes so that you see just one picture, not two.

To get the correct and best view from merging two pictures into one, you have to adjust the lenses on the binoculars. To do this, you look through the left eyepiece (which is always locked) at some object and then you move your center dial to get that object in perfect focus. Then you look through your right eyepiece, which is adjustable, and turn its dial until it is also in perfect focus with the left lens. You lock that position in and then squeeze the two tubes together until you have one picture in perfect focus. Finally, you turn your center dial further or closer to get the picture all in focus.

I handed him back his expensive binoculars I had just "fixed" and he said, "Well, maybe instead of Davy Crockett, I'm more like Elmer Fudd."

To which I replied, "We were all rookies once. No shame in being a rookie."

Keeping the right focus is like using binoculars. To stay focused on the important, you use your impact as the object you're focusing on. You use the left eyepiece of your core values that don't change to focus in on making sure you're acting within those values. You look through the right eyepiece, which is those people in your circle of trust who will help you refine your focus to match your values and get your impact into sharper focus. Finally, you bring these two lenses together. It will give you one picture with clarity.

The next step is to decide how far you want to look. Do you want to see objects which are close to you or those that are far away? That is where your goals and measurements come in.

KEEP THE CORRECT SCORE. MEASURE IMPACT, NOT TIME.

Your weight, height and temperature are the health measurements that matter in your early years. Then, as you grow older, your blood pressure, cholesterol, blood sugar, and many other measurements start to matter. Most of you know what these numbers are now. If you're being treated for a specific illness, there are likely even more specific numbers that you are watching carefully. Do you know the thickness of your fingernails or hair? Probably not, because these numbers seldom tell anything about your health.

In life and business, as in our health, we need to know what numbers to watch and what goals to set in order to truly determine our health and our impact.

Continuing with the binocular analogy, when I got my first set of binoculars for outdoor sports, I used them to see more clearly objects that I had already spotted. This was very helpful and fun. Then I started using my binoculars to see things way in the distance that I could not see with just my eyes. I suddenly saw more deer, turkey, and a variety of wildlife than when I just zoomed in on the few things I could see first with bare eyes.

Once you have used your values and trusted friends to focus your view on your impact, you can then decide what you need to measure. You can determine which of those should be close to you and which should be far in the distance. Whether close or near, you then need to focus on them to get that clarity.

Setting goals and measuring impact for ourselves, versus the organizations we are in can be a challenge, especially when we are starting with the end in mind. For parents, it's a bit easier as we start by just wanting our children to be healthy and happy. Then we move into education, sports, and life goals, while always praying for health and happiness. If you defined your impact after Chapter One, try to put that into a number.

"I want to improve people's lives." How many people in your lifetime? Dozens, hundreds, thousands, millions? How deep of an impact on each life? Like the ripple effect in Chapter One, will you have an immediate, direct, deep impact or a more distant, shallow impact?

If you want children to learn to do math, do you want to be a classroom teacher who enlightens them one at a time and sees the joy or pain in their eyes? Or do you want to write a computer math game that touches the lives of many students who you never see?

Do you want to provide quality prescription drugs efficiently to millions, like my friend Dave Bernauer did as the chairman of Walgreen's? Or do you want to be like his friend? He owned his one local drug store and helped thousands get prescription drugs and advice over his counter, all while looking them in the eye and knowing about their lives and families?

As you think through this matrix of close or far, deep or deeper, many or fewer, it will help shape how you can measure your impact on people. It will also help you shape your destination. As in my case, it may change as the journey changes from very close, direct, and deep to global and deep, but not direct.

As you determine your measurement tools and goals, make sure that you are not evaluating the thickness of your fingernails, but the numbers that truly measure health and impact. Hours and dollars spent are input measurements, not impact measurements. The actual measurable results are the impact. Consider how much more effective our governments would be if they measured success by results versus resources used; e.g., the number of students who are learning vs. money spent on education, the number of people moved out of poverty vs. the amount of money spent to fight poverty, military readiness and combat performance vs. dollars spent.

THE NUMBER OF HOURS YOU SPEND AT WORK IS NOT YOUR IMPACT. WHAT YOU ACCOMPLISH IS YOUR IMPACT.

Measuring the wrong things can also take you off track. Once I had a very good executive working with me as a fundraiser. The day he walked into my office and told me how many days he had been on the road that year, I knew he would be leaving soon. He asked me how many days I had been on the road and I couldn't tell him because I never counted. When he told me he hadn't counted either, but his wife had, I knew for sure that his days were numbered. For him and his family, getting off the road was the right direction. I was already a road warrior when my kids were born and had built my family life around this reality. I learned that it was very difficult for others to become road warriors mid-career or stay road warriors when they started growing families.

In your life there are negative numbers you can measure. Just like the volcanic rocks that can cut you if you run your bike into them, focusing on the negative numbers will, at the least, slow you down and may well wreck your journey all together.

When fishing in Alaska with Jack Shewmaker and Jack Kahl, we would end the day over dinner with everyone regaling us with their stories of the day. Everyone would talk about how many fish they had caught and how big they were. When asked how many fish or how big a fish he caught, Jack Shewmaker would reply, "I think I saw a fish." He had come to the point of knowing that the number and size of the fish were not the best ways to measure this experience. Thanks to Jack, I no longer count the fish I catch or the hours on the water.

SUMMARY:

- ☞ Don't let the immediate get in the way of the important. Use the two lenses of your virtual binoculars to determine the immediate and the important.
- ☞ The number of hours you spend at work is not your impact. What you accomplish is your impact.

ACTION STEPS:

- ☞ List 10 important things you need to achieve. Then use your "binoculars" to identify the top three and list them in order of priority.

CHAPTER NINE

BRING PASSION AND ENERGY.

To honor their roots, and to help keep the downtown square in Bentonville, Arkansas alive, Sam Walton and Walmart decided to build a museum of the company history in the building that was originally the Walton Five and Dime store. I was privileged to be invited to attend the opening and dedication ceremonies, as were the entire state of Arkansas and every Walmart customer in America.

The square was closed for the dedication, and a stage had been set up on the street right in front of the museum. As with any Walmart opening at that time, the stage was a flatbed semi-truck trailer covered with red, white, and blue bunting and Walmart signs borrowed from Walmart logistics. The ceremony began and the local dignitaries all spoke. Then some of Walmart's top leaders spoke, and the governor of Arkansas spoke and played his saxophone.

Following the opening ceremonies, Sam Walton took the stage. He thanked everyone, including the governor, and said, "Remember the name Bill Clinton. I think our governor has a bright future ahead of him." Just as Sam Walton began to speak, it started to rain. It was a slow drizzle at first, and then it became a steady rain. There was Sam Walton holding a wired microphone standing on the steel floor of a steel trailer in a pouring rain. Don Soderquist, the vice-chairman of Walmart, grabbed a large golf umbrella and held it over Mr. Walton. This didn't work so well because Mr. Walton walked all over the stage as he talked, and he kept bumping into the much taller Soderquist who was trying to keep him dry.

Finally, after a few minutes, Mr. Walton stopped and looked at Don and said, "Don, don't bother with that umbrella. I burn off the rain." The crowd burst out laughing. Sure enough, Sam Walton was so inspiring to us all that he burned off the rain, not only from himself but from us. We stood and listened and ignored that we were getting soaked to the bone.

For me, this story epitomized the passion Sam Walton carried, not only on stage but every day as he went to work. Even during my last meeting with him, riddled with cancer though he was, his eyes sparkled, and his weakened voice carried that passion. Mr. Walton was passionate about helping ordinary people do extraordinary things. He was passionate about helping everyday folks and less fortunate folks save money so they could live better lives and make life better for their children. He was passionate about America, democracy, and free enterprise. He burned off the rain!

Today I believe we are giving our young people the wrong advice. Too often, we say, "Find what you are passionate about—make that your work and you will be happy." My experience has been that those who are Accelerator Leaders bring their passion for life and people to whatever they are doing.

I remember watching my father at the boys' ranch repairing a broken sewer pipe with such gusto and energy that every boy there willingly grabbed a shovel and dug into the stinking ditch until we could find the broken pipe and replace it. No one woke up that day and said, "Gee, I want to go dig up a stinky sewer pipe today." But because of Dad's passion to "get the job done, no matter how dirty the job is," everyone pitched in and we soon stopped all the pollution.

Jack Kahl, the king of Duck Tape, wasn't born with a passion for rolls of gray tape. He had a passion for life, people, innovation, and serving customers. He got into the duct tape business and brought his passion with him. He took a drab gray tape from the commercial market to the consumer market, added hundreds of colors and patterns, and made it a cultural icon.

I was there in Alaska when camouflage duct tape was invented on one of our fishing trips. Jack's passion is why so many people were willing to swim the dirty water of the retaining pond to celebrate his latest victories, as mentioned in Chapter Five.

You need to bring your passion and energy to the impact you're having now and let it shape the impact you will have in the future. At times a person's passion doesn't and can't match his or her career. My friend Jeremy is a great IT guy whose deepest passion beyond family is fly-fishing. He will fish all night, sleep for a couple of hours, then go to work and never skip a beat. At times we would discuss how he could make a living at fly-fishing. Even though he worked for me, I enjoyed these discussions that might cost me my great IT guy. We even looked into a potential fly-fishing resort as a business opportunity.

In the final analysis, Jeremy always came to the same conclusion: if he made fly fishing his career and his family's financial well-being depended on his ability to catch fish or help others catch fish, it would take all the fun out of fly fishing. Whether or not he had a good day of catching fish would now matter to his paying clients and his reputation as a guide, outfitter, or resort owner. He made the decision to bring his passion to his IT work to increase his value and paycheck. That way, he could provide his family with even more financial security while enjoying fishing as his diversion from work.

LET YOUR PASSION SHOW, QUIETLY OR LOUDLY.

While Sam Walton's and Jack Kahl's passion was always evident by their exuberance, not all Accelerator Leaders are as outwardly expressive. One of the most effective ads and posters we used at Enactus showed two well-known CEOs with their faces painted with our logo and shouting like the biggest sports fans in the world. The ad worked so well because both of these CEOs were noted for their quiet calm leadership and not for great exuberance.

We got many calls from other CEOs who said, "If David Bernauer, CEO of Walgreen's, and Doug Conant, CEO of Campbell's Soup, are this excited about your organization, I have to come and see it myself." Dave and Doug were both passionate leaders who showed their passion in quiet ways. Both were passionate about developing people into better leaders. Dave was also very passionate about finding new and better ways to get things done to deliver better value, service, and health care to customers. Doug was passionate about developing leaders and organizations that were built on purpose and who proved you can do well by doing good. Everyone who worked with them knew and felt their passion just as much as those who worked with Sam Walton and Jack Kahl. In all these cases, these leaders' personalities reflected their passion. All of them brought their passion to their family, work, and hobbies.

When you bring your passion to your impact and to every facet of your life, other people will follow you. Quiet or with exuberance, they will follow.

SUMMARY:

- ⟳ It's more about bringing your passion to what you do than searching for your passion.
- ⟳ Others will follow those who have passion and energy in their life.

ACTION STEPS:

- ☞ Determine how you can better share your passion in your work and life.
- ☞ Develop a plan to manage your energy so that you can function at full energy when needed.

CHAPTER TEN

TAKE ACTION. GET MOVING, BUT SET THE RIGHT PACE.

When my brother, Randy, and I were teenagers, working on the farm, the family car was a big blue Buick LeSabre with four doors that very comfortably seated six adults. Compared to the Mustangs, Camaros, Chevelles, and Firebirds, it was not very impressive as a cruising car, but it was all we had. However, one advantage was that it could hold a lot of people, so we sort of made it the party car for taking lots of people to fun places.

On one of the rainy days when we couldn't work the fields, a bunch of us decided to go to the big city of Springfield, Missouri, forty miles away, to go to the drive-in movie. We gathered a car full of guys and gals and off we went. We filled up at the gas station on the edge of town. My good buddy, Ryan, who was a bit of a rebel—always pushing the limits, decided he wanted to sneak into the drive-in without paying by climbing into the trunk. My brother and I were preacher's kids, so we seldom crossed the line. When we did, we feared the wrath of God and, even worse, the wrath of our father. Even so, we relented and let our friend climb into the trunk.

As we rode to the drive-in theater, the rain hit really hard. When we pulled up to the ticket booth the lady said, "I can't sell you tickets." Oh no. My brother and I looked at each other, knowing we'd just been busted for our freeloader in the trunk. We were going to have to face the wrath of our father. "Why?" we asked.

"A tornado just touched ground on the west side of town and is coming straight this way and will be here in 30 minutes," she said. "All the cars in the theater have to leave now so you can't come in." Just then the tornado sirens kicked in everywhere. Now we knew we were going to face the wrath of God. There we were in the big city, away from home. We didn't know where to go or what to do and everyone started screaming and yelling at the same time. We turned the radio to the best weather station. I shouted, "Shut up!" and told my brother to drive north.

We hit the street just in front of all the traffic coming out of the drive-in, driving toward the main highway. My brother headed north. Everybody in the car quit screaming so we could listen to the radio, because that was the only way we could track the tornado. This was true for everyone except our friend in the trunk, who could only hear the sirens; kept beating on the trunk; and yelling for us to let him out. We couldn't stop to let him out and still get to safety. The tornado kept moving due east while we headed north. Within 30 minutes, it hit the drive-in. The place was so badly damaged it never reopened. By then we were forty miles north. Within minutes, we were home, safe and sound. We let Ryan's sister open the trunk. Ryan jumped out, ready to fight, until she told him that we had just saved their lives. He calmed down a little.

I doubt that the action we took will be written up in any storm warning guide, but based on what we knew, we made the best decision we could and saved several lives. What we knew was that the tornado was to our west and moving straight east. Home was north, so to get out of its path, going north to home was better than south to nowhere.

I knew that that the big old four-door Buick had a GM V8 engine with 454 cubic inches of muscle fed by a four-barrel carburetor. I also knew my brother was a better driver than me or anyone else in the car, as proven by unofficial races in that big old boat of a family car that ate Mustangs and Camaros all day long. (More than once, our dinner dates were paid for by Pony car drivers who thought they could beat our big blue Buick. After the race, we ate steak while they ate our dust. And on occasion we were the ones taking their dates home.) With this limited data, it was easy to make a sound decision quickly and take action. We had confidence in our destination and our ability to execute, while not taking action could have meant death.

Fast forward 25 years. Tom Moser was elected vice-chairman of the Enactus board, which would move him to chairman the next year. He is the vice-chairman of KPMG, an auditing firm. We met to discuss what he wanted to accomplish in his term as chairman. He was starting with the end in mind: "What will my legacy be as chairman?"

KPMG is in almost every country in the world. Enactus is in six.

Tom's goal was to "Make Enactus a global organization." His question: "How?"

I shared our idea of doing a global competition outside the United States. It would take us five years of growth to get to that point. Currently, the national champions from the six countries have attended the Enactus International Expo in the U.S. and competed with all of the 150 plus USA regional champions. The international teams got lost in this crowd, and the event looked and felt very American and not very global.

"Great concept," says Tom. His colleague, Bernie Milano from the KPMG foundation, agreed. "Let's do it next year in London."

Bernie's jaw dropped and I almost fell out of my chair. I gave Tom a long list of why we needed five years to get ready—number of countries, funding, global donors, etc.

"Next year in London," Tom repeated.

"Okay," I said, "Why London?"

"It's a global city. KPMG has a strong practice there and the royal family is a client. We can get them to host a dinner in Kensington Palace, where the princes live, and where Princess Diana once lived. That will attract top CEOs. We'll start a special campaign to recruit event sponsors at $50,000 each in new money and KPMG will be the first. Right, Bernie? Alvin," he said, "I will go with you to meet with Lee Scott, the CEO of Walmart, and we'll ask him to co-chair the host committee. We will do the event whenever he's going to be in London. Once he agrees, we'll recruit top CEOs to join the host committee and be sponsors. I will go to the KPMG network and work with my colleagues in other countries to get Enactus started in at least 10 more countries. My London colleagues will use their meeting planning team to pull the event together."

It felt like the tornado all over again. Think fast. We knew the impact we wanted to have. We knew it fit our core values and strategic plan. Tom clearly was the best driver you could find. Not to mention, he was now going to be my direct boss.

"I'm in," was my only possible response.

Tom took it to the board for approval and we announced it at the Enactus International Expo to the entire community just two months later. Tom delivered. Lee Scott said yes. So did a dozen other top CEOs. The VIP dinner was held in Kensington Palace. The KPMG network helped start Enactus in over a dozen countries and we had 12 countries compete at the first World Cup. The final judges were a panel of global CEOs. The CEOs were so impressed, they signed up their companies to join KPMG and Walmart in taking Enactus global.

Due to Tom Moser, the potential tornado turned into a very favorable trade wind that carried us for several years. Who knew an auditor would be such an Accelerator Leader?

An Accelerator Leader takes action. The tornado sirens are going off, people are in a panic, and you don't have time to collect and calculate perfect information. You must make a judgment on the spot, where and when to take action. General Norman Schwarzkopf, Allied Commander of the Gulf War in his book, *It Doesn't take a Hero*, says the first rule of leadership is **when put in charge, take charge**.

Some people are so action-driven they argue that instead of "ready, aim, fire" it should be "ready, fire, aim." I disagree. I believe the best approach is to be ready, aim quickly, and fire with precision. It is taking information you can get in the time that you have to make the best decision possible and then be decisive. Once you decide, then go with it full bore, and bring everybody else along by convincing them quickly with conviction and confidence. To be an Accelerator Leader, you have to take action and be decisive. Your confidence in your decision should encourage everyone else to follow.

You also have to adjust fast. Think about it. It's much faster to change the direction of a car, boat, or plane when it's moving than when it is sitting still. Take action, get good feedback, and adjust as needed.

OBSTACLES TO TAKING ACTION

There are many obstacles to taking action, and I've come to the conclusion that, at their core, they're mostly issues of pride, which can also mean fear of failure. One of these is the "paralysis of analysis." I don't remember right now which book coined this phrase, but it's very much to the point, especially in today's world full of data analysis and massive computing power. Because we can get access to so much data, we often delay action until we get one more data point, and then one more data point, and then one more… Then nothing happens or it happens too late.

The second big barrier to action is the need for perfection. There are those who want everything to be perfect. They want the stars to align. They want the perfect shade of blue. They want a guarantee of a perfect outcome. By waiting for perfection, what they usually get is the perfect storm. The perfect they are looking for is a delusion. Life is never perfect. People are never perfect. Short of heaven, there is no perfection; we are human beings, and we are imperfect. If you seek the perfect, you will always be disappointed, and you will always delay your actions.

Instead of seeking perfection, seek excellence. Do the best you can, but always look for the better way. Is there a better solution or better direction? Are there better people? Are there better choices? Not perfect, but better. Take the best you can and look for the better. If you're constantly looking for better, you will actually increase your quality, because you will be moving towards what might be the perfect solution. Don't seek the perfect, seek the better.

The third barrier to taking action is not wanting to look foolish. I shared with you the story of Jack Shewmaker inviting me to go with Sam Walton. I turned it down because I didn't know how to shoot shotguns well and I didn't want to look like a fool. It looks like doing nothing is safer than doing something and failing or looking bad. Fear of failure actually tends to drive leaders more than the desire for success, but it can also lead to paralysis and inaction.

Remember the story earlier about when Sam Walton wore the grass skirt and did the hula on Wall Street? By looking silly, he made it clear to all of his associates that: 1) He didn't take himself too seriously. 2) Business can be fun. 3) It's okay in our company to take a risk even if you might look foolish at the time – but deliver the impact.

If you focus on reaching your peak impact, there's no room for inaction or paralysis or egos. You should ask yourself, "Am I interested more in doing good than looking good?" Then take the action that results in the most impact.

Colonel Daniel Shewmaker told me that pilots have an expression, "That guy's all thrust and no vector." That means that the guy is going nowhere fast: too much speed and no direction. **Accelerator Leaders take action, knowing where they're going; are guided by who they want to be; and determine who they want to greet them when they cross the next finish line.**

What are the actions you need to undertake now to start on the path to becoming an Accelerator Leader? Do you need more education? Better relationships? A different job? Different contacts?

SET THE RIGHT GOALS; KEEP THE CORRECT SCORE

Once introduced to The Indy 500, I became a bit of an addict. To enable my addiction, my good friend and board chairman, Stanley Gaines, arranged tickets for me and my family, along with VIP treatment for several years. Stanley was involved through his business, GNB, originally Gould National Battery. GNB was owned by a major conglomerate and Stanley was the CEO. When the conglomerate decided to sell GNB, Stanley and the management, with a group of investors, bought GNB through a leveraged buyout. After unshackling from the parent company, Stanley ran GNB like an entrepreneur and it grew like crazy. He bought the rights to the Champion brand name for batteries and offered it to Walmart as their exclusive brand. Bingo! Sales jumped even more.

Stanley introduced me to Roger Penske, a great entrepreneur and owner of one of the top Indy 500 car teams. I asked Roger what it took to win the Indy 500 and other big races. He answered, "The Indy 500 is never won on the straight-away, with the throttle wide open, where the finish line and checkered flag are. It's actually won in the curves and in the pit stops. If you don't slow down and take the curves at the right speed and angle, you crash into the wall or your opponent passes you. If you don't take the right amount of pit stops at the right time and with the right speed, you don't win."

Just as in the Indy 500, **to achieve the legacy you want and to maximize your impact, you have to learn when to put the pedal to the metal and go full bore; when to slow down for the curve; and when to get off of the track to refuel and get new tires.**

TAKE TIME FOR PIT STOPS

One regret in my career is that I did not spend more time off the track with my family. Early in my career, Enactus was in a grow-or-die phase, so responding full bore all day every day seemed to be the only choice. I continued this pace even after we got over the survival hump and moved to the growth phase. Bob Rich helped me best understand how to set the right pace. Bob was chairman of the Enactus board. He was also president of Rich Products out of Buffalo, New York.

Bob had taken a company, which his grandfather founded and his father built, into a whole new level of growth around the world. Yet, Bob also had the time to be a very accomplished angler. He fished with a lot of famous people, President George H. W. Bush for one, in the world's best fishing places. I envied his fishing prowess and complained to him one day about wishing I had more time to fish so I could get as good as he was. His response was a very unsympathetic, "If you don't have time to fish, it's your fault, not your job's fault. You either don't have the right team; don't trust them enough to do their jobs; you're not organized enough; or you aren't setting the right priorities." Ouch!

"Okay," I replied, "It's all my fault so help me fix it." He did so through great mentoring.

Get your priorities right. Use your binoculars and set annual, multi-year, and long-term goals that are aligned with your legacy. Of all the choices you must make in a given day, week, month, or year, which ones align with these goals and which ones move you closer to these goals and have the biggest impact? There are several resources to help, like Steven Covey's *Seven Habits of Highly Successful People*. Jim Collins' concept of the "Stop Doing List" in the classic book *Good to Great* applies to you as well as to your organization.

Discipline. Body builders (and I'm not even close to being one) know that muscle growth happens on days of rest, not during the actual stress of the workout. Discipline yourself to take pit stops as needed. Refuel, get new tires, get a drink of cool water, check the engine. Then, when you get back on the track, you can, in fact, go faster and have more impact. If you don't, you will run out of fuel or blow a tire or an engine. When this happens on the track, it usually not only means that you end the race way behind the others; it often means you crash and never get to the end.

To make time for pit stops, you have to discipline yourself to hit your goals and get your work done in the allotted time. To do this, you need to measure the right thing—impact, not time, which can be the wrong thing. Too many of us measure our work by hours spent vs. impact. If I focus on impact, I can get the essential work done in less time than if I focus on how many hours I spend on something. As a young manager, I erred in evaluating people by the hours they spent. I thought those who came in early and stayed late were better workers than those who punched the clock. They had a better work ethic. As I matured and started focusing on impact and not inputs, I learned that many of those who came early and stayed late had less impact. They came early and stayed late because they were not disciplined enough to focus on priorities, and they also wasted a lot of time during the day hanging out at the water cooler or break room. I found others who came early and stayed late who *did* have great impact and discipline. I also found that some clock watchers were unproductive, while others were very productive. **Measure your impact, not your time. Do the same with others.**

Donna Patterson had just been promoted to chief global development officer. I had a very long heart-to-heart conversation with her about all the work she needed to get done and when in her new role. Our relationship and this conversation were such that she felt open to sharing transparently and honestly. Her response was, "I can't do everything you want me to do in the time you want it done. But no one else, including you, could do it either. What I can do is tell you what I can get done, and in what time frame, and I can guarantee you that I will deliver better results than you asked for. Give me my expected impact and let me decide the best way for me to get it done." I agreed, and she knocked it out of the park.

WHAT IF YOU CRASH?

Thanks again to my friend Robert Campbell at Valvoline, I was back at the 1989 Indianapolis 500 with my son, Ben. My family had become hooked on IndyCar racing. Ben was only five years old, but already had a favorite driver, Al Unser, Jr., who drove the Valvoline Car. Robert arranged for Ben to meet Al, Jr., by having Ben wait in the hall of the hotel, right outside the VIP Banquet room. As Al, Jr., approached the room, Robert introduced young Ben. Al, Jr., shook hands let us take a picture, and autographed a picture for Ben. Needless to say, when the race started, Ben was yelling loudly for his (even more) favorite driver.

The race is 200 laps around a 2.5-mile track. We were seated in the bleachers near the finish line. We could see the cars head into Turn One and approach Turn Two. The backstretch and Turn Three were out of view. Then we could see them enter Turn Four and race down the front straightaway and past the finish line. We watched lap after lap after lap. When the drivers were out of sight, we kept an eye on the electronic leader board. At Lap 198, Al Unser, Jr. took the lead from Emerson Fittipaldi. We cheered loudly as Al Jr. sped through the straightaway in front of us. Our excitement rose, knowing he had only two laps to go to get the checkered flag. We watched intently as he rounded the first turn, then we were fixated on the leader board as he sped out of sight. He emerged neck-and-neck with Fittipaldi as they approached the fourth turn. We watched in disbelief when we saw Al Jr.'s and Fittipaldi's wheels touch. The Valvoline car spun out of control and hit the wall. Fittipaldi made the last lap around the track under the yellow caution flag. As Emerson carefully passed the wrecked car, Al Jr. gave him a thumbs up and Fittipaldi crossed the finish line to victory. Al Jr. showed real class that day, but there was no joy in Mudville, or for the Rohrs family.

There may come a time in your career and life when you crash and burn and have to be towed to the garage. The crash may be your fault, because you made the wrong choices and decisions. The crash may be the fault of someone else who made the wrong choices and decisions that affected you. The crash may be due to things so big and overwhelming that you don't know whom to blame.

No matter what or who caused the crash, it's up to you to decide what you do, once you are in the garage. You can rebuild the car, learn from your mistakes, get back on the track and win the race the following year like Al Jr. did, or you can quit and throw yourself on the junk pile and have no impact. The choice is yours. Some of us need more time in the garage, rebuilding, than others, depending on how hard we were hit. An Accelerator Leader will not only get back on the track but will rebuild in a way to have even greater impact.

Life happens. Your career may veer off course or crash. You may get towed to the garage. Put yourself back together and learn from the crash.

Accelerate yourself and get back on the track. You just might have an even bigger impact than if there had never been a crash.

The next step is to maximize your impact by accelerating others.

SUMMARY:

- When put in charge, take charge.
- Don't seek perfection. Instead, seek excellence.
- Accelerator Leaders take action, but they do it after knowing where they are going. They are guided by who they want to be and who they want to greet them when they cross the next finish line.
- Know when to speed ahead, when to slow down on the curve, or when to stop to refuel.
- Measure your impact, not your time.

ACTION STEPS:

- ☞ Identify three of your top impact goals and write them down in terms of excellence vs. perfection.
- ☞ Look at your calendar and schedule time for pit stops to refuel and to be in the garage for repairs.
- ☞ Develop a system to measure your impact vs. your time.

PART TWO

ACCELERATE OTHERS

---

*Life is a sphere of interconnected
personal and professional relationships
where you can influence others to
accelerate their impact and yours.
People will constantly come and
go in and out of your life and your
organization. Maximize acceleration
while they are part of your sphere.*

Life is a sphere of interconnected personal and professional relationships where you can influence others to accelerate their impact and yours. People will constantly come and go in and out of your life and your organization. Maximize acceleration while they are part of your sphere.

Leonard Roberts, retired chairman and CEO of RadioShack, told me about an interesting event in his early career. He was a mid-level manager at Ralston Purina in St. Louis and had been given the assignment by the chairman to design Ralston's first incentive-based compensation plan. It was the beginning of détente with the Soviet Union and the U.S. State Department had organized a trade mission so the Soviets could learn about our agricultural system. Len was assigned to meet with a mid-level bureaucrat in the Soviet government and explain to him how the incentive compensation system worked.

Len put together a great presentation on the new plan Ralston was implementing. For an hour, he explained to this mid-level bureaucrat how incentive compensation works. After the presentation, the Soviet guest responded with, "Thank you. Great presentation. Now tell me how the whole thing works."

Len responded, "I told you everything about our new compensation system. From top to bottom."

"I mean the whole thing. What is an incentive? What is a market? How are prices determined? How do incentives affect how resources are allocated? How is profit an incentive? The whole story. How does America's market economy work?"

This was way beyond Len's assignment and time allotment, but he decided to dive in. He went back mentally to his Econ 101 class in college and drew supply and demand charts, then moved on all the way to how the fractional banking system worked. It took hours and then his guest left.

I asked Len if he knew whether his econ lessons did any good. "I hope so," he replied, "That mid-level bureaucrat's name was Mikhail *Gorbachev.*"

Maximize others' acceleration while they are part of your sphere. Family, friends, colleagues, and acquaintances are all in your sphere. You never know when it will lead to great impact.

CHAPTER ELEVEN

ACCELERATOR LEADERS ARE MASTER GUIDES

At a business event I attended that was organized by my good friend, Jesse Turley, one of the recreation choices was fly fishing on the Provo River. I was paired with a new acquaintance, Steven Hirth, and was assigned a guide for the afternoon. We climbed into the guide's truck and headed to the river. This looked very promising. The truck was full of the right gear, worn a bit, but not so old and worn out you wondered if he made any money at this.

The conversation was all good and, obviously, the guide knew trout, this river, and fly-fishing. We got to the river, and the guide started to rig the rods. "What fly are you putting on?" I asked.

"It's an XYZ," he replied, "I invented it and sell it to two of the major fishing retailers."

The voice in my head went, *oh, crap!*

"Do you have any other flies you invented and sold to them?" I asked.

"No. This is my only baby."

Oh, crap, went that voice again.

I knew what would happen and, sure enough, it did. All afternoon we used his baby. No matter the water speed. No matter the weather. No matter what bugs were in the water. We used his baby. I used my best techniques learned from years on the water. I caught two fish all afternoon.

My new friend, Steven Hirth, on his first ever fly-fishing adventure, caught none and never even felt one bite. Time was up. We loaded in the truck and headed back to the gathering place. "Tough day," said the guide. "The water was high, and the weather just wouldn't cooperate."

"That's too bad," Steven responded.

I knew better.

We got to the gathering place. Every other angler, rookie or old pro, had caught fish and one of the groups slayed 'em, catching at least a dozen each. Steven looked at me and said, "It wasn't the weather or the high water, was it?"

"No. I knew what was going on and I should have demanded the guide change our flies, but I just very seldom go against a guide's advice," was my reply. Bad news: bad fishing. Good news: a new friend. I'll take a new friend over any number of fish. When I told my friend Jesse what had happened that day, he made sure that guide never showed up at any of his events again.

A much different outcome happened in West Virginia. I was standing in the river, watching a beautiful rainbow trout move toward my fly. Just as he opened his mouth to grab it, I jerked the line to set the hook and jerked it right out of his mouth, ripping his lip. At almost that same instant I felt a big slap on the back of my head. Bam! My guide had smacked me just like my momma used to when I was really bad.

"That was a trout, not a bass. You lift the rod, not jerk the rod, when landing trout. It is subtlety, not muscle. This is the tenth honey hole you blew, and you will NOT rip the lips of MY fish any more. Is that clear?" he yelled.

Normally, a fishing guide will not slap you on the head or get in your face and yell at you. This was no ordinary guide. This was a master guide – Sir Robert Rich, Jr., owner and chairman of Rich Products, past chairman of my board and angler extraordinaire, as mentioned earlier.

This was also no ordinary river. This was the fly-fishing venue at the Greenbrier, a gorgeous and exclusive resort in West Virginia. Sir Bob and his angler wife, Mindy, owned a house on this river. Members only and their guests got to fish the river. These fish were, in fact, Sir Bob's fish and I had been ripping their lips all morning long. It was very clear that the next ripped lip would be my last cast in this river and maybe the last time Bob would spend this amount of quality time with me.

We moved to the next honey hole and Bob once again explained to me, "Use this fly because of this water and what the fish are eating in this hole. Cast your fly there, mend your line just so. Let it drift. Wait, wait! Now lift—don't jerk—the rod."

Bam, on the line was a beautiful rainbow.

I landed it, released it, and Bob gave me a big slap on the back. Much better than a big slap on the head. The trip down the river continued, honey hole to honey hole. Each time, Bob gave fewer and fewer instructions and then no instructions. Finally, Bob said, "Fish on down to the house and I will meet you there," and he left. My first thought was Bob was tired of me, and then it occurred to me that he left because he had taught me all I needed to know to fish on my own. He was a true master guide. He made himself dispensable.

Become a master guide.

I have had many guides on my fishing and hunting expeditions. There are bad guides, okay guides, good guides and master guides.

A bad guide will take your money, go through the motions and couldn't care less if you are successful. They have another source of income or plan to quit guiding at the first chance possible. Some use guiding to let you pay to cover the cost for them to fish. An okay guide will help you catch fish in the easiest way possible, but if it doesn't work, it's not his problem. He just wants to make sure you don't give him bad reviews. These okay guides usually make their money on one-time tourists who never come back.

A good guide will work hard to get you on fish and make sure you have a good experience: good conversation, good food, plenty of water, etc. He wants a good review. A great guide will bust his chops to get you on fish and will get you rigged up with whatever gear, fly, or lure will work to catch any fish possible so that you will hire him again and recommend him to your friends. A master guide like Bob Rich will teach you how to fish so that you never need another guide again.

Accelerator Leaders are master guides: to accelerate others, to help them see their own potential, to help them equip themselves to succeed, and to help them become self-reliant.

You know you have been a good master guide when you start learning from your former pupil and when they start accelerating you.

TEACH THEM THE WHY

Why fish there? Why use that fly? Why that casting technique here and another one there?

To become a master guide, you have to go past the "what" and the "how." You must remember the words of my vocational Ag teacher, Mr. Hood, "The person that knows *how* to do something will always have a job. The person that knows *why* will always be the boss."

Not only must you seek and learn the why to accelerate yourself, you must help others understand the why. With a child, it's easier to tie his shoes than it is to teach him to tie his shoes; but in the long run, it's best that he learns. If you want him to make sure that his shoes stay tied, he also needs to learn the why. If your shoes are untied, you will trip and fall, or lose your shoes. Once he gets it, he will keep them tied. Sometimes we have to let them lose their shoes or trip and fall before they finally get the why.

"Where," "what," "when," and "why" are the basics of learning. The difference between a great guide and a master guide is the focus on the why. **Accelerator Leaders are always about the why; finding it and helping others discover it.**

SEE THEIR POTENTIAL

The best anglers in the world started out as rookies. Master guides remember where they started. They know from personal experience that others can become as good as they or even better.

My first face-to-face meeting with Jack Shewmaker was on my turf. He was invited to speak to a large group of college and high school students on the campus of Southwest Baptist University. Jack gave the most inspiring and compelling speech I had ever heard. As we left the auditorium and headed to the dining commons, I asked Jack to become the chairman of Enactus. He said yes, but wanted to get Sam Walton to approve. A few days later Jack called and said Sam wanted to support Enactus and approved Jack serving as chairman. Jack then invited me to his office to discuss what this meant.

My first meeting with Jack Shewmaker in his office was very memorable for me. I arrived at the Walmart home office, which looked like a warehouse, because it had been. I spent 30 minutes finding a parking space, then walked into the visitors' waiting area. I was amused that the paneling on the walls was the same as that in a mobile home I had lived in for a while as a kid. Bud Walton, Sam's brother, had fish mounts on the wall of all the big native and exotic fish he had caught over the years. I went to the receptionist's desk and signed in, got my name badge, and found a seat in the crowded room full of vendors. Shortly after, Jack came into the room and shook my hand. He bought us both a nickel cup of coffee and then we went to his office. It was small and plain. The walls were covered with family photos and memorabilia, awards and accolades from the industry, along with accounting sheets.

I asked him why he had agreed on the spot, during our first meeting, to be the chairman of Enactus. To be honest, I was hoping he would say something about what a great guy I was, but that didn't happen. "It's the students. When I saw them, I saw me. I was born and raised in Dallas County, right next door to Polk County. I came from a good middle-class family, but we still didn't have much. I had friends who lived in houses with dirt floors who grew up and succeeded. I believe if we give children the right education and let them live in a free country with free enterprise, they can truly grow up to be whatever they want to be. When I see those students, I don't see who they are, I see who they will become. I think what Enactus does will help them reach that, more than any other organization I've seen."

He pointed to a needlepoint on the wall behind his desk and said, "Helen Walton made this for me because this is one of many things Sam and I totally agree on."

It read, *"Treat people as if they are who they are and that is who they will be. Treat people as if they are what they can become and that is who they will become."*

SEE THE BEST, FIND THE BEST AND BRING OUT THE BEST IN OTHERS

I grew up with great examples of this in my parents. They raised boys at boys' ranches and group homes who had been abandoned or given up on by society. My father, the son of an abusive, alcoholic father and ill-tempered mother, grew up with people around him who discounted his future because of the "family dysfunction" of his parents. However, thanks to the many men and women—relatives, teachers, coaches, preachers—who stepped into his life, he was helped to see his potential. He made a career out of helping boys whose futures seemed bleak to find their best selves and to become good fathers and husbands.

In this era of massive data and algorithms to solve every issue, I am concerned that many employers have moved too far down the path of using computers to do their hiring. Computers can match experience and, to some degree, personality traits, but I doubt there will ever be a logarithm to predict true potential.

Seeing the potential is difficult.

Having been a volunteer youth soccer coach, I can testify that most parents have trouble evaluating their children's true potential at an early age. Millions of parents think their children are bound for the World Cup. However, the reality is that extremely few of these children will ever get there. They know their children's capabilities from years of raising them, watching them, and teaching them. Even then, we often get it wrong. I have also seen the opposite: parents who belittled their children into thinking they were useless or almost trash. Victims of emotional, verbal and physical abuse find it difficult to see any potential, much less their full potential. Those who do often had someone other than their parents step in, just like my parents did for over 1,500 boys.

Who in your life were the people who saw your full potential and encouraged you to keep reaching and striving? Your parents, a few teachers, a college prof, a coach, mentors, a boss? How did they see it and how did they help you? That is what master guides do with others.

It starts by how you look at them. I don't in any way condone the behavior of the man in this next story, but it's one life lesson I learned from a bad source. To pay for college, I worked many different jobs. One of those was as temp labor for an agency in Kansas City. For several weeks I worked at a factory in the inner city. It was hot, dirty work. The factory had large dipping vats full of boiling hot chemicals. The inside was so uncomfortable that, to cool off on break and lunch, we went outside and sat on the hot sidewalk in July.

The owner was an obvious bigot. You did not have to be around him long before his language and word choice made it clear that he had very strong opinions about people who were different from him. Color, race, ethnicity, gender, religion—his words hit them all. Mostly I just avoided him, as did the other workers. One day I happened to be sitting on the sidewalk, cooling off. The owner's office A/C had broken down, so his window was open. I overheard this conversation with his plant manager.

Owner: "Our business is growing like crazy, but we can't fill all the orders. What's the problem?"

Plant manager: "I can't find enough workers to fill a second shift, much less start a third shift."

Owner: "Why not? We're in a part of the city with high unemployment and these are low-skilled jobs."

Plant manager: "I've hired all the white guys I can find."

Owner: "What do you mean?"

Plant manager: "I know what you think about people, so I only hire white men."

Owner: "You $#*!#, what color are my customers?"

Plant manager: "I don't know?"

Owner: "They are all GREEN! When I see them, I only see the color of money. I don't see their skin color or race or gender. When I look at workers, I see them the same way. They are all GREEN, the color of money. If they're willing to work in this sweat box, show up on time and do their jobs, I couldn't care less about their color, sex, race, religion or anything else. Go find me all the GREEN people you can and let's run this plant at full capacity 24/7."

I was shocked that an obvious low-minded bigot could actually have one spark of enlightenment. His comments challenged me. Did I really see people as green, not necessarily the color of money, but the color of opportunity? Did I see them for who they are or who they could be? Did I judge their potential from their past or from their future? Did their external differences or similarities to me shape my view of their potential?

Growing up, I often heard that you can't judge a book by its cover, because what's on the outside doesn't matter; the only thing that matters is on the inside. My experience is that this isn't true. What's on the outside *does* matter. **Seeing a person's full potential isn't about looking past their external flaws or how they're different from you. It is about seeing them as green. It's about seeing them as a person of potential and understanding how their external and internal realities can help them reach their full potential.**

One person's flaw may be another person's best asset. What you or they perceive as their flaw may in fact be an asset. I shared earlier how my inability to use my hands in shop class drove me to make sure I went to college. My brother's incredible ability to use his hands and brain to make and fix things drove him to a great career as a mechanic. It's a bizarre example, but I know a guy who has no sense of smell. He makes a nice living cleaning up places where no one else wants to go. His biggest asset is a nose that doesn't work!

When you start looking for the green, the potential in people, you will see them in a new light. You can help them do effective personal evaluations and grow their self-awareness. You can help them find their strengths and improve their weaknesses.

Their past or present does not determine their future unless you let it.

EMPOWER THEM TO DISCOVER THEIR OWN POTENTIAL AND IMPACT.

Accelerating others isn't about lighting a rocket up their rear ends, as one of my good friends always suggests. It's not about scripting their futures, as too many parents want to do these days. **It is about helping them on their journey of self-discovery and helping them expand their self-awareness.**

I have traveled over four million miles by airplane in my career. I have spent a lot of time sitting by people, which means I should have a lot of people that I have helped accelerate. Unfortunately, most of that time was spent with my headphones on and a mask over my eyes—either sleeping or pretending to sleep. I have spent as many as 16 hours with some people, but it was not acceleration time. Just being physically close to people, engaging in daily chit chat, casual conversation, or rubbing shoulders with them at work is not acceleration time.

To accelerate others, you must invest in them. You can't help them reach their full potentials from a great distance or through a written evaluation form. **The scarcest and most valuable resource you have is your time. You must invest it in those you want to accelerate.** For example, invest it in your spouse and children, other family and friends, and your colleagues at work. To be a master guide, you have to spend time on the water with those you want to accelerate.

Just as in the story of how Jack Shewmaker helped me discover my potential at fly fishing, you can help others by using the snapshot, video, and mirror.

As a kid, I loved to fish, but seldom got to fish with my father, for two reasons. One: my father was a wonderful man, but he was a workaholic. He did not know how to pace himself. We seldom took vacations or even days off. He wanted to help as many boys as possible, so he could never say no to a boy who needed our home; we were always above capacity and lived on stretched resources.

Second: if we did go fishing, any boy who wanted to go got to go, too. Of course, we never had enough fishing rods, so inevitably my rod went to one of the younger boys. Consequently, most of the fishing I did in my youth was done alone or with a few other boys. I had a fishing rod that came in five pieces, so I could hide it up my shirtsleeve, sneak off to the farm pond, assemble it, and fish, with no one else knowing I was going fishing. If any other boys knew where I was going, I knew my dad would make me take them, and, again, my fishing rod would become theirs.

After my father retired, and then moved to a care home with Mom, I made it a point to take him fishing. There was a small lake at their care home, with a gazebo extending over the water. I would wheel Dad out to the gazebo so that we could fish over the railing.

As his Parkinson's got worse, this became a challenge. Part of this horrible illness included a growing dementia. It progressed to the point where, to fish, I had to bring a bar stool out for Dad to sit on. It enabled him to fish over the railing, since he was no longer able to stand up. On one trip, my dad hooked a fish and tried to stand up so that he could move along the railing to land the fish. I kept saying, "Dad, please don't get up. If you fall and hurt yourself, the home won't let me bring you out here to fish anymore."

This scenario repeated itself three or four times until Dad actually fell.

I picked him up and got him back onto the stool as fast as possible, so that no one inside would see and come stop us. I got in his face as he had done to me many times growing up and I said, "Dad, do not stand up again or we'll have to stop fishing forever."

He looked at me with tears and said, "Son, I'm so sorry, but I can't remember that I can't walk."

My heart broke and my eyes filled with tears. We went back to fishing. Now, I put my rod down and stood behind Dad and spent the rest of the day helping him catch fish. Each time, I gently reminded him to stay on his stool. We would land the fish and he'd say, "This is the biggest fish I've caught all day."

"Yes, it is," I would reply, knowing that it wasn't, because I knew he couldn't remember the size of any other fish he had caught. That day I truly lived "in the moment" with my dad. Every cast was his first cast, every fish was his first fish and every fish was, in his mind, the biggest fish he had caught in his life. It reminded me of a powerful lesson I knew, but too frequently practiced—being truly present with someone. Unfortunately, because of his health, it was the last time we went fishing. I hate that damned Parkinson's disease.

Investing time means meaningful time. I have done far more acceleration of family, friends, and colleagues at breakfasts, lunches, dinners, campfires, soccer games, and playing Pretty Pretty Princess than I have in my office. **Be present in the moment. Make it about them and not about you. Get past the task of the minute to the moments that matter.**

HELP THEM PLAY UP.

It's human nature to stay in our comfort zones. Once you guide someone to the point of them reaching success—high batting average, getting straight A's, always delivering on time, on schedule, and on budget—it's time to help them play up. To look for better. To move to the next league.

In the movie *Bull Durham*, there is a scene where the lead actress has just discovered that her boyfriend, a veteran player, is about to set a new record for home runs in the minor leagues. She is ready to go to the press and make it a very big deal. The boyfriend says, "No, being the best home run hitter in the minor leagues is not what I want to be remembered for." He still had the dream of moving up to the big leagues, even as distant as that seemed in his current career.

Give them bigger and bigger challenges. The biggest challenge is knowing when to encourage them to move to the next league. How do you know for sure they are ready? There is no *sure*. Given a choice between ready or not ready, err on the side of encouraging them upward. If they are ready, they will soar. If they aren't ready, they may fall flat. If they do, that's okay. It gives them a chance to learn and then to pick themselves up and try again. To help them pick themselves up, you have to give them the freedom and permission to fail. If you encourage them to play up, they have to know you have their back. They have to know that if they soar, you will rejoice with them, and if they fail, you will be there to help them get back up again.

Don't expect a home run hitter in the minor leagues to hit a home run the first time they're at bat in the majors. Expect a strikeout and be there to help them get back in the batter's box the next time, and the next time, until it's finally a major league homer. **If you do not give them permission to strike out at times, and you don't help them get back**

up and into the batters' box, you will crush them, and they'll never see their full potential, much less reach it.

Bob Plaster made very generous contributions to Enactus. In his honor, we named our new building The Robert Plaster Free Enterprise Center. I asked Bob to make remarks at the dedication ceremony. Reluctantly, he agreed. Bob told me he was okay speaking, but not comfortable speaking in public. He then went on to tell me how his father had died when he was fifteen years old, in the depths of the Great Depression. His mother worked hard to take care of the family and he helped all that he could as well. As a kid he was very shy. He would never raise his hand to answer a question and definitely would never stand up in class to make any presentations. "Mom made sure we wore clean clothes every day. But those clothes were all hand-me-downs and they all had patches. If I drew any attention to myself, the kids would make fun of my patches. So, I kept my hand down and never stood in front of the class."

He then shared that when he joined the National Guard, his sergeant saw his leadership potential. The sergeant assigned Bob to teach the other cadets artillery lessons. Bob responded that he didn't know anything about teaching, so the sergeant gave him the teacher's book and said, "Read this and teach this. You're a leader and a teacher. Now go do it."

Standing in front of the class in his uniform with no patches, Bob taught the lesson and soon moved up to the next leadership position. That sergeant saw Bob's "green" and forced him under orders to play up. Once Bob knew he could lead, he went on to do great things. I asked Bob what drove him so hard to build his business and amass his wealth. Bob's response was, "I want to make sure I leave enough to my family so that none of my children, grandchildren, and descendants have to wear clothes with patches." That was his way of saying that his impact was to protect his family from poverty like he had experienced in the Great Depression. It is a force that I've seen drive many in his generation.

During the first year of my career, I attended the national convention of the Association of Private Enterprise Education (APEE), a gathering of academics who held chairs of private enterprise or free enterprise on college campuses. The elite scholars of market economics attended and presented their latest research. I was the rookie and was there to become familiar with the group and help advance the organization I led.

It became very evident early on that Mary McCleary Posner was the guest of honor. She was not an academic but was the CEO of her own public relations firm in New York City. She was working with the APEE and had secured a grant from a major foundation to fund the publication and distribution of a series of journals titled *The Future of Private Enterprise*. This provided a significantly larger platform and audience for the APEE scholar's work.

Because she was the rock star of the event, it was a bit challenging to get close to her as many scholars were vying to get their work published in her journals. Finally, I managed to sit at her table for a luncheon on the second day. In my introduction I mentioned that I lived in Missouri. She immediately leaned in and told me that she was originally from Columbia, Missouri. When I told her I was a recent graduate of the law school at the University of Missouri in Columbia, she said, "My father was the dean of the law school for many years. Have you heard of Dean McCleary?"

Heard of him? He was a legend. He was the dean that put our law school on the map as the dominant one in Missouri; we were nationally recognized because of him. "Everyone knows about Dean McCleary," was my response. There was a magical connection, and we were instant friends. After lunch, she invited me to join her sightseeing around the convention's host city, Washington, D.C. We grabbed a cab, and I got a great guided tour.

I asked Mary why she didn't go into law since her father was so prominent in the legal field. Her answer shocked me. "At the time I entered college," she replied, "my father told me that good grades in law school, even with his high-level connections, wouldn't get a woman hired at a major law firm. He suggested that my best path to reach my potential, as a woman, was business." She then told me how she had gotten her degree and moved to New York. She set a goal to be the CEO of a public relations firm by the age of forty. She told me about her many successes and the struggles of climbing the ladder in a big city agency. She also told me about the glass ceiling she kept hitting.

Eventually, Mary decided that the only way to achieve her goal of being a CEO by the age of 40 was to start her own agency. She did just that and went on to great success. I was very impressed that a young woman from the small city of Columbia, Missouri had made it big in New York. I was familiar with the lyrics to "New York, New York," written by Fred Ebb and made popular by Frank Sinatra: "If I can make it there, I'll make it anywhere." She had conquered the Big Apple.

I shared with Mary that, after the convention in D.C., I was heading to New York for one of my first business trips. She looked me square in the eyes and said, "No offense, but they are going to eat you alive." Mary was very polished and sophisticated, yet very street savvy. Apparently, she didn't think this country boy was ready for the Big Apple quite yet.

Over dinner, Mary schooled me on all things New York. She started with geography: Uptown, Downtown, Midtown, Soho, Upper East Side, West Side, and the Financial District. She taught me where they were, what to avoid, and what to enjoy. I learned that streets run east and west and avenues run north and south. She also let me in on why Central Park is a big deal, how to hail a taxi by knowing what the lights on top of the car mean, and which parts of the city were safe. I asked her how to use the subway and she responded, "You are not ready to try that." Then she moved on to what to talk about and what to avoid talking about. Then she taught me some New York speak, especially some phrases that are often used that a Midwesterner would not know. She even told me how to get through LaGuardia Airport and come out alive.

When I arrived in New York, I was much better prepared and much more confident. I also had Mary's phone number as back up. The week in New York went very well. I landed several new donors and went home singing "New York, New York." Mary continued as my master guide in

New York on my future trips and made many introductions for me. She recognized my potential, but also saw where I needed improvement. She taught me the *whys* of New York: why people acted the way they did, and why they thought the way they thought. She spent the quality time required to guide me to the point where I no longer needed her phone number as a security blanket.

Mary became an active supporter of SIFE, now Enactus, and joined the Board of Directors, where she served for many years. She became good friends with fellow board member Robert Plaster, and currently serves as a trustee of the Robert W. Plaster Foundation.

Several years after we met, Mary and her husband Allen decided to move back to Missouri. Their client base was very solid, and they could do their work from home. They created one of the early versions of a virtual company. On her return to Columbia, Mary became aware that the local school kids didn't have a very good grasp of the price that veterans and others had paid to ensure their freedom. She was concerned that Memorial Day was just another long weekend for vacations and shopping with little remembrance really being offered. She decided that she would make Memorial Day one of the biggest days of the year in Columbia and teach the children why they had freedom.

By that time in my career, I had become successful at fundraising and she wanted to learn how to raise funds for her new venture. It was now my turn to become her master guide. I taught her the why of donors' motivations to give, the why of proper donor recognition, and, most importantly, the why of building quality relationships with donors who would eventually see themselves as members of the organization, not just donors to the organization. We spent a significant amount of time working out the plan and discussing potential donors. Mary executed the plan flawlessly and raised the money to get it started. In year one the celebration was comprised of a small local parade and an airshow. It soon grew to become the largest free admittance airshow in America and one of the biggest Memorial Day weekend events in the nation. Mary's fundraising ability went way beyond what I had taught her. Because of what she had done in Columbia, she was asked to serve on the commission that designed and funded the National Korean War Memorial in Washington, D.C. If you want to be truly inspired, go to the Air Show for the Memorial Day weekend (it is now held in Jefferson City, Missouri) and make sure you visit the Korean War Memorial on the plaza in Washington, D.C..

Mary's role as my master guide for the urban jungle of New York City is a great example of what you can do for those you are accelerating. Teach them the why, see their potential, empower them to achieve their potential and help them play up. Who knows, you just might find a time when someone you guided becomes your guide.

SUMMARY:

🔹 Accelerator Leaders help others see their own potential, help them equip themselves to succeed, and help them become self-reliant.

- ☞ Find the why and help others discover it.
- ☞ See others as green. See their potential and understand how their external and internal realities can help them reach their full potential. The past and the present cannot define their future unless they let it.
- ☞ Invest your time in those you want to accelerate. Be present in the moments that matter.
- ☞ Give others permission to strike out, and if they do, pick them up again.

ACTION STEPS:

- ☞ Make a list of your work colleagues, friends, and family. Evaluate your list based on seeing their green vs. how you've seen them in the past.
- ☞ Make a list of five people you will invest more time in.
- ☞ Who on your list needs to play up? Determine how you can help them do so and how you will still have their backs if they fail.

CHAPTER TWELVE

ACCELERATOR LEADERS ARE SHEPHERDS WHO INSPIRE

You can't push a chain. This basically means that you really can't motivate people who don't want to be motivated. It's one of those lessons you are given early in leadership positions that you think you've learned until you find yourself once again trying to push a chain. When I hear this expression, I'm always reminded of watching the movie *Ben Hur* as a kid. It made a great impression on me.

One of the most compelling scenes is when Ben Hur is a slave on a Roman galley, rowing to the beat of a drum, shackled in chains. As Ben Hur's ship approaches the enemy ships, the drum beat gets faster and faster, louder and louder, as they row faster and faster and faster and then CRASH! They ram the enemy ship. Water floods the rowing chamber and it's every man for himself. Prisoners struggle to get out of their chains. They turn on their captors and kill them to get the keys. Those who are able to flee for safety. The shackles and pounding hammer might have kept the ship moving in smooth waters, but when turmoil and trouble hit, there was no loyalty, no teamwork, and certainly no sacrifice. Death yes, but no sacrifice for others.

Have you ever worked at a place and for a boss that felt like this prisoner-powered war ship?

Contrast this to the leadership style in one of my favorite poems, the 23rd Psalm: "The Lord is my Shepherd; I have all I need. He lets me rest in green meadows; He leads me beside peaceful streams. He renews my strength. He guides me along right paths, bringing honor to his name. Even when I walk through the valley of the shadow of death, I will not be afraid, for you are close beside me. Your rod and your staff protect and comfort me. You prepare a feast for me in the presence of my enemies. You honor me by anointing my head with oil. My cup overflows with blessings. Surely your goodness and unfailing love will pursue me all the days of my life, and I will live in the house of the Lord forever."

As the shepherd on my farm growing up, this poem always spoke to me. Did you notice the "leads me" phrase? The difference between a sheepherder and a shepherd is whether the sheep are in front or behind. Sheepherders drive, while shepherds lead. Joined with the verse in John 10:27, "My sheep listen to my voice; I know them, and they follow me," we get an even more complete picture of the shepherd.

The ecosystem of a flock of sheep is built on trust. Sheep aren't just animals who follow blindly. Each is a unique creature with its own personality, but each one was also created with a herd instinct. They learn to trust each other. When the flock is grazing calmly, a constant hum of bleating from one to another lets the flock know everything is alright. When any sheep senses danger and starts to run, they all run without question. The entire flock responds as a cohesive group because each sheep trusts the others to protect it from danger.

The shepherd leads the sheep because they trust him. The sheep hear his voice and they know that in the past he has led them down the right paths to green meadows and peaceful streams. The shepherd has used the rod to protect them from enemies; he has used the staff to gently keep them on the path and safe from harm. **The sheep follow because they trust the shepherd and are inspired by the shepherd to know that their lives will be better and safer by following him.**

The job of a shepherd is not just to watch the sheep. The real job of a shepherd is to convert forage, grass, and weeds that humans can't eat or wear into protein and wool humans can use. The job of a shepherd is to help the sheep grow as much wool as possible and gain as much weight as possible. To do that, the shepherd must lead them to still waters where they can drink all they need and then to green pastures where they eat quietly and contently with little stress until they are full. Then the shepherd lets them lie down in those green pastures to chew their cud and digest the delicious grass they just ate. You can drive sheep to green grass and water, but the driving creates stress. In contrast, leading the sheep gets them there with little to no stress. When wolves or wild dogs attack, the shepherd uses his rod, a short, stout club, to beat them off. Using a club means close quarters, in-your-face fighting. The shepherd uses his staff, a long cane with a hook on the end, to guide the sheep to the right place. A gentle tap here or there keeps them moving or changes their direction. If the sheep try to go where there is danger, the shepherd grabs them with the big hook of his staff and pulls them back.

Accelerator Leaders are like pilots guiding the plane and all inside to a destination, speeding forward at 500 mph, but letting the passengers feel safe and have a smooth ride. To do this, Accelerator Leaders need to be shepherds. The environment and ecosystem you create need to be like the still waters and green pastures. The environment needs to let your colleagues be fully productive to reach their full potential. While the green pastures give a picture of the ultimate serenity, your environment is not likely to be serene.

Sheep are prey. They have multiple stomachs. In the wild they go into open grass fields ever watchful for predators. They eat fast and fill up the first stomach which is like a storage tank. Then they go find a safe place to hide, still watchful for predators. There they lie down and retrieve food from the first stomach, which becomes a wad of grass that they then chew more finely—this is called a "cud." This finely processed grass now goes into the second stomach where it can be digested. Sheep with a shepherd don't have to graze in fear. They can eat in peace, and when full they don't have to go hide; they can lie down right in that open pasture and fully digest their food in peace. Because of this peace, all their energy is used to grow wool and protein; none of it is wasted on watching predators or hiding from them.

People need action and activity to be productive. To focus their energy on being productive, they need an environment that they know is safe where they can work in relative peace. They need to know that you have their backs, that you will protect them from external and internal attacks, that you will not run from danger, but will use your rod of authority to battle for them even if it means engaging in hand-to-hand combat if necessary. **If they know they can trust you, they will focus on work and not worry.** Your colleagues also need to know you'll lead them with your staff of authority. You will find the best path forward and guide them gently with your staff, rather than beating them over the head with your club. If they get off the path, they know you'll use the crook to pull them back onto the path and give them the opportunity to go back to being productive.

HOW DO YOU SHEPHERD?

Say thank you in the right way

"Say 'please' and 'thank you'" are words I grew up with.

The words "thank you" are two of the most powerful words that accelerate others. Saying thank you in the right way makes them even more powerful.

Doug Conant, founder and chairman of Conant Leadership, former CEO of Campbell's, former chairman of Avon, is a legendary leader. He is legendary for always saying "Thank you." His book *Touchpoints* is the best text for saying "thank you" in an inspiring, Accelerator Leader way. He has handwritten tens of thousands of personal notes: "thank you" notes, congratulations, inspirational messages, and friendly greetings. I have kept every one ever written to me in my safe. They are valuable and treasured because they are genuine, relevant, timely, and personal. Each note was written when he was focusing on me in the moment. His handwritten notes are masterpieces of examples on how to say "thank you."

I did not and do not say "thank you" enough, in part because I don't expect to be thanked. I enjoy it when I am, but my attitude is, "I have a job to do, so I do it without needing praise." Sometimes my ego gets in the way. It lets me take too much credit for success without acknowledging those who really made it happen—something I continue to learn.

To overcome this, I've tried to duplicate Doug Conant's approach of using hand-written notes. Unfortunately, my handwriting is so bad, people can't read what I have written. Worse, they might think that I had hired a third grader to write them for me. The best I can do is write a personal note in a birthday or work anniversary card. Doing this, I have found that it makes me focus on the person being thanked and makes me really appreciate what they have done to improve the company's impact. I now make it a point to say "thank you" in specific ways to let them know they are appreciated.

I've come to understand that saying "thank you" in the right way means three things: 1. Being genuine about what you say and how you say it. 2. Only saying thank you when it is genuinely deserved. Don't blow smoke. 3. Saying thank you in the way each person wants to be thanked.

I try to get to know people well enough to understand whether they need a pat on the back in private or in front of others, a personal note, accolades on stage, or just a quick email or text. Some people hate being fussed over; some want to be fussed over all the time. Some people love the spotlight on stage and are motivated by the chance to get back on stage. Some people hate the spotlight on stage so much that if they get it, they'll make darn sure they don't do anything to have that happen again.

Accelerator Leaders say "thank you" in the right way.

BUILD AND GROW YOUR FLOCK

Attract, retain, and inspire those with the most potential (those with the most green) who best fit the culture.

The first step in building an effective team in your organization is seeing the green in each team member. See each one through the lens of her potential, rather than through the lens of her past or present. Each member of your team is one in seven billion.

The second step is to ensure that each team member and his potential fit your culture. Organizations want to hire the best talent, so when they find that great talent, they bring that person on board, regardless of fit with the culture. The honeymoon usually ends quickly. The great new talent either fights the culture, creating division internally, or he spends so much time trying to fit in that he is no longer a great talent. That person often ends up leaving or being pushed out.

How someone fits the culture is not about whether he or she is a good person. It's not about whether he or she is talented. It is simply about whether, do they fit. If so, bring on their green. If not, let their green go where they can reach their full potential in an organization where they fit.

RECOGNIZE WHAT YOU WANT TO BE REPLICATED

Incentives work because they create an internal competition for people. They ask themselves, "Can I reach that goal and get the prize, the incentive?" Recognition is one of the best incentives. To achieve your organization's maximum impact, recognize what you want replicated. **Recognition of positive impact is far more effective than punishing bad outcomes or behavior.** You still need to use corrective action when required, but if your culture is one where people get punished more than praised, you're not achieving your maximum impact. Instead, you are likely experiencing a lot of churn in your ranks.

Every organization needs to measure many things to understand their success and to know how to allocate resources, but not all of those factors should be used as incentive goals. **Incentive goals should be based only on those numbers that create the greatest impact.**

Saying "thank you" is recognition. You need to recognize people in the way they want to be recognized. You need to offer incentives people want. At Enactus, when we tried to incentivize people by giving them a day off for a specific achievement, it didn't work. My HR leader said, "We can't get the people here to take all of their vacation. Why would offering them a day off they won't take motivate them?" Great question. Recognize people the way they want to be recognized by offering incentives that are valuable to them.

PEOPLE SUPPORT WHAT THEY HELP TO CREATE.

Let others share, grow, and shape your dream beyond what you thought possible.

Robert T. "Sonny" Davis, the founder of SIFE, made this the core of the leadership training he developed and then brought into SIFE, which is now Enactus. My first SIFE experience was a training retreat in St. Louis led by Sonny. He had built into the event great free enterprise education materials and experiences that featured the power of teamwork and participative management. These ideas are standard now, but his work was ground-breaking in the 1970s when most organizations and companies were managed under the military style of top-down decision making. For the college students of the 70s like me, this made SIFE even more attractive. In the post-Vietnam era, we all thought we needed a voice in everything. SIFE was built on engaging students to learn, do, and teach. This message empowered us as students.

Don't just tell people what to do. Teach them the "why," then ask them what should be done. Take lots of input. **The final decision or direction will not agree with everyone's input, but if you received input from everyone, those whose ideas were not adopted are far more likely to eventually support the new decision or direction than if they were never asked.**

CULL THE HERD

Being a shepherd also requires culling the herd. There are those sheep that are more productive than others, and there is a limited amount of grass and water. As the shepherd, when I was growing up, it was part of my job to decide which sheep to move out by selling, which to keep, and which new ones to bring into the flock. I remember Mr. Hood doing a site visit on my farm for my FFA project. He brought some of the freshmen to watch and learn. He looked over my flock of breeding ewes (the females) and noticed two in particular. We had just sheared them, so they had no wool and were very exposed. One was nice and fat, while the other was so skinny it made you wonder if she was going to survive.

"Which one of these should he keep, and which one should he cull and sell?" Mr. Hood asked the freshmen.

"Keep the big fat one," they all replied.

"Alvin," he asked, "which one are you keeping?"

"Watch this," I said as I opened the gate to the lamb pen. All the lambs ran to their mothers to nurse. There was Miss-Fat-and-Pretty with no lambs, and there was Miss

Skinny with three lambs nursing. "The skinny ewe has had triplets for three years," I explained. "All the food she eats goes to make milk for her babies. The fat ewe hasn't had a baby for two years so all the food she eats only goes to make her fatter. I'm keeping Miss Skinny," I concluded. Despite the appearances, the results made the decision easy.

As you make decisions about who to keep, who to move out, and who to move up, use the data and measurements that really matter—not the appearance of performance, but the actual performance.

Encourage the mavericks but remove the renegades.

Maverick – an independent-minded person or an unorthodox person. Renegade – a person who behaves in a rebelliously unconventional manner, a person who deserts and betrays an organization or set of principles.

In my flock, I had one ewe that was always looking for greener grass. While most of the sheep were content to just keep their heads down, she would wander around and look for new sources of food. She was one of my favorites because once she found new food, the others would move to her. As a result, all of them found better food and did not graze the original field to the point that it killed the grass. She was a maverick.

I had another ewe that also kept looking for greener grass, but she was not my favorite. When the flock was led to a new pasture, instead of eating this new greener grass, she would run directly to the new fence and run around the entire circumference of the field looking for a hole in that fence. If she found one, she would squeeze through it, and soon the others would follow. If she couldn't find a hole big enough to squeeze through, she would find whatever hole she could and push into it more and more, enlarging the hole until she finally got through. Since she was a fairly productive ewe, I tolerated her.

One morning I went to let the sheep out, only to find this ewe had once again broken a hole in the fence and led the flock out of the safety of the pen. When I finally found the flock, to my horror they had been attacked by dogs. A fourth of them were dead, a fourth were maimed, and the rest were scattered and running around, frightened and bleating for their lambs. The troublemaker was one of the survivors. I cleaned up the horrible mess, then I did what I should have done months before. I loaded up the renegade ewe and took her to the market. Never again did I tolerate a renegade in my flock, no matter how productive it appeared to be. This ewe's rebellion destroyed the flock and caused the death of other sheep.

In my work, I've found that encouraging mavericks who want to try new things and come up with new ideas can be very valuable to the organization. Many times, it's the mavericks who find the new greener grass and make things better for everyone. However, if that independent spirit becomes rebellious, refuses to accept the mission of the organization, violates its core values, or makes it a point to always reject leadership just to reject leadership, that person needs to be cut out of the herd, regardless of how valuable he or she might appear to be. If you don't move that person on, he or she will hurt others and damage your organization.

Accelerate others through inspiration, not through commands. Lead, don't drive. Words of inspiration are very important. Your flock must know your voice and trust your voice. Actions speak louder than any words. If the shepherd leads the sheep to bad grass and dry streams, or runs away when the wolves come to attack, the sheep will no longer follow. No words of inspiration will get them to follow the next time.

How you live your life and how you conduct yourself at work is what is the most inspiring. If you genuinely care for those in your circle of influence, help them see their full potential. Let them know you want what is best for them. Help them find how they can have their own impact. Explain how joining with your impact multiplies theirs. Through these processes, you will inspire them.

If you inspire your flock, they will follow you places where you could never drive them to.

If you truly inspire people, they will even follow you through the valley of the shadow of death.

Sylvester John, the head of the Enactus International Division, asked me to meet with him and two of his top leaders, Yusuf Majidov and Zohra Zori, to share a big idea with me. I agreed and then asked, "What's this big idea?"

"We want to launch our organization in Afghanistan," was Sylvester's response.

"What, are you crazy?" I asked in shock.

"We are deadly serious," was their joint reply. Then I stopped and analyzed who was standing before me. Sylvester John is a native of Sierra Leone, educated in Ghana, and a graduate of North Florida University. As an Enactus student at North Florida, he had established Enactus in Ghana as a project. We then hired Sylvester as our first regional leader to launch Enactus in Africa. The Enactus model was very different as we were building self-sufficient national organizations.

When Sylvester told his parents about his new position, they were very proud. When they asked him how much money each country was going to receive from the USA headquarters, he told them, "None." Then they thought he was crazy. He explained his plans to teach country leaders to raise their own funds in their own countries. "That is not how it works in Africa. You are doomed to fail," his parents replied. Because of his good work, we opened 12 countries in Africa. Three of the most financially successful country operations in the network at the time were in Africa—Egypt, Nigeria and South Africa. At that time, they were each raising more money than most of the country operations in the developed world.

Yusef Majidov was one of the pioneers who launched Enactus in Central Asia. He helped organize the first competition outside the USA. He owned his own private college but decided to give it up to become the full-time Central Asia regional leader for Enactus. During his tenure there was much political turmoil in that region. He spent most of his time travelling from country to country, building a self-sustaining organization in each. He has many stories to tell of border guards and other officials wanting bribes. His refusal to pay led to a few broken bones.

Zohra Zori was born in Afghanistan. I called her our *Sound of Music* girl because of her family's incredible story. Her father was a general in the Afghan Army and her mother was the Minister of Health in Afghanistan when the Soviet Union invaded. The Soviets told her father that if he led the army in support of the Soviets, he could retain his title and all their possessions and lifestyle. But if he refused, they would kill his family. In the middle of the night, Zohra's older brother grabbed her from her bed and they joined the rest of the family as they escaped over the mountains of Afghanistan, just like the von Trapp family in *The Sound of Music*. Through several relocations, they eventually landed in Jacksonville, Florida. Her mother worked as a nurse. Her father, once a general, had to work as a janitor. Eventually, the family saved enough money to open a restaurant and become entrepreneurs. Her parents made a courageous and costly decision.

Zohra enrolled at North Florida University in Jacksonville. She had not yet found her calling and didn't feel like she fit in anywhere. She was recruited into the Enactus Team and found her impact. After graduation, she joined the Enactus USA staff as a regional rep, starting and coaching Enactus teams. She was soon promoted to the International Division. Now, standing in front of me at this meeting, Zhora was the head of our International Program Department.

I realized that, if anyone could launch our organization in Afghanistan, it was these three. "Tell me more," I asked. We all sat down, and they gave me the details. There were several agencies in the United States and Europe who were going to fund the rebuilding of Afghanistan after the war. Their plan included helping Afghans start micro-enterprises, as well as encouraging university students to become entrepreneurs and to help others start micro-enterprises. That is exactly what Enactus does. It was exactly the kind of impact we were practiced at making.

They laid out their plans. Yusef already had connections at the universities in Afghanistan, just as he had in all the other "stans" in Central Asia. Zohra had family in Afghanistan who could help us get government clearance. She had a family friend, a businessman in Afghanistan, who had already agreed to provide some of the seed money. Sylvester had his connections in the U.S. State Department who verified this businessman's credentials as being legitimate.

"Can we apply for these grants?" they all asked at the same time.

"There's one major hurdle," I replied. "Afghanistan is still a war zone. If we do this, all three of you will have to travel to Afghanistan often. Every time you go, you run a very high probability you will be shot and killed. I'm sorry, but I cannot ask you three to take a bullet for this organization" I cautioned.

These three stood before me: Sylvester John, a survivor of more than one armed rebellion in West Africa; Yusof Majidov, who was still healing from his last border-crossing beating; and Zohra Zori, who had fled her homeland as a child and wanted to return to help save it.

"You are not asking us to take a bullet. We are asking you permission to allow us to take that risk," said Yusof.

"We are willing to take that risk," they responded in unison.

"Okay. Send in the applications," I answered. I felt this had to be my answer. "If we do this, I'll join you there whenever you need me. I will not ask my team to take a risk that I won't take as well," I committed.

I realized that they believed so much in our impact and what it would do for the people of Afghanistan that they were willing to risk their lives, to walk through the valley of the shadow of death. I also realized that they weren't following me, I was following them. Because of who they were and what they had already accomplished, I was ready to let them be my shepherds. The applications went in, but unfortunately, conditions in the war got worse and all these plans had to be dropped. There was no opportunity to succeed. Maybe we could come back and fight again another day.

Accelerator Leaders are shepherds who inspire.

SUMMARY:

- ๕ Others will follow you because they trust you and know their lives will be better because of you.
- ๕ Say "thank you" in the right way.
- ๕ Recognize what you want to be replicated.
- ๕ Lead, don't drive.

ACTION STEP:

- ๕ See yourself as a shepherd. Determine what your rod and staff will be, and how you can build stronger trust with your team.

☞ Develop a list of 10 people you need to say "thank you" to and determine the right way to say "thank you" to them. Then do it!

☞ Identify those achievements and behaviors you want your team to replicate and develop an appropriate recognition system so that those behaviors will be replicated.

PART THREE

ACCELERATE YOUR ORGANIZATION

Develop a sustainable impact. Build
a river, not a reservoir. Build a
replicable, adaptable, and scalable
organism that will be sustainable.

Develop a sustainable impact. Build a river, not a reservoir. Build a replicable, adaptable, and scalable organism that will be sustainable.

In my high school years, I was watching football with a bunch of the boys from the Good Samaritan Boys Ranch in Missouri on a very rainy Sunday afternoon. Billy, one of the boys at the ranch who had opted to go fishing instead, barged into the room yelling, "The dam is breaking! The dam is breaking!"

"What dam?" my father asked, trying to figure out if we had a dam.

We had had several days of rain, which was nothing unusual.

"The front pond dam," replied Billy, "The water is about to go over the top of the dam."

The pond was only about an acre in surface area. It had been there for years and was built with a spillway that would allow significant amounts of run-off before the water was ever high enough to come over the main dam. It had been so reliable, we took it for granted.

We all rushed to the pond and saw that Billy was right. The water in the pond was running out of the spillway at full capacity and was rising to the top of the dam itself. We realized that if we didn't do something very quickly, the water would go over the main dam and it would create massive erosion, which would break the dam. The barns and other farm buildings that were below the pond were at risk. If the dam broke, the wall of water would destroy all of our buildings.

The good news was that we had a built-in rescue crew: the 65 boys who lived at the Boys Ranch. We ran to get old feed sacks and began filling them with sand. We started an assembly line that quickly filled the bags, loaded them in the bucket of the tractor, and transported them to where they were needed. Another assembly line unloaded and stacked the bags in just the right places. While we were working, the rain stopped so we could see that with each layer of sandbags added, we reduced the threat of the flood. After a few hours, we had a dam on top of the dam. We knew it was now safe.

On the farm, that pond was a calm body of water. We never really thought about it being dangerous. What we didn't realize was that weeds and brush had grown up in the spillway to prevent a smooth flow of high water. We also found out that, over the years, silt had filled the bottom of the pond, making it shallower every year and reducing its capacity. We thought the stability of the pond made it safe and that having the pond there removed the threat to the barns and other buildings in the original flood plain.

We make the mistake of thinking stability results in sustainability. We think we can build solid structures like dams that will harness nature and make us eternally safe. With our organizations, we build buildings, systems, processes, and bureaucracies, thinking that we are building stability, thinking we are building a dam that will stop the river and that will lead to sustainability. Then in comes the 10-year or 100-year or 1000-year flood that shows us how feeble we really are. We get blindsided by our competition, customers change their minds, the disrupters hit, and the dam breaks and wipes out everything we built up over many years.

The reality is that life is fluid. The Earth itself is fluid. The continents are continuously moving. The magma at the earth's core is constantly pushing upwards, shooting out of volcanoes. Why do we delude ourselves that building what we think are solid structures on shifting ground creates long-term sustainability?

If you want to build an organization that is sustainable, build one that is fluid.

CHAPTER THIRTEEN

WHAT DOES A RIVER ORGANIZATION LOOK LIKE?

In Search of Excellence was published in 1982, the year I became CEO of SIFE. It was the first blockbuster business book and is one of the all-time best sellers. I read and studied it as I began my journey with SIFE. The authors made the case that too many companies saw themselves as the wrong thing and let other opportunities pass them by. One example was railroads, which saw themselves as just railroads and not transportation companies; therefore, they saw trucking and other forms of transportation as competition and let others take over those markets. Eventually the railroads almost died. The book also emphasized how change is constant and companies must be adaptable. Although it was written in 1982, even today, too many organizations are still acting like the old railroads.

Building a river means building an organization that is replicable, adaptable, scalable, and sustainable.

BUILD THE STREAMBED AND BANKS, THEN FILL THEM WITH WATER THAT CREATES AN ECOSYSTEM.

All analogies eventually break down, but the analogy of the river works for me. A river is made up of the bed (or bottom) and the banks (or sides) and the water. A river bed is usually bedrock as the water has eroded the soil down to bare, solid rock. The banks are what gives the river its shape. Without water, the bed and banks are just a ditch. Water is what gives life to a river. The water is filled with fish, animals and plants. The water also attracts other animals and plants to the banks to drink and grow, making up the ecosystem of the stream. Human activity such as fishing, transportation and irrigation are also a part of this ecosystem.

The river ecosystem is fluid, always moving and always in flux. Just like the water that flows down a stream, products come and go, services come and go, people come and go, and customers come and go. If you dam the stream and think that you will permanently preserve or retain products, services, people, or customers, you are only deluding yourself. The big flood will eventually come, and the damage will be far worse than the damage from any normal river flood. If you do succeed in building a dam and reservoir that traps everything permanently, your reservoir will be like the Great Salt Lake that has no outlet. It fills itself with salty silt as the sun evaporates the water. It will become full of salt and unable to sustain life.

CULTURE IS THE BEDS AND BANKS. PROTECT YOUR CORE VALUES AND GUIDING PRINCIPLES. CHANGE THEM INTENTIONALLY AND GRADUALLY.

When you look at an organization, it is the culture of the organization that defines its shape, just like the bed and banks define the shape of a stream. The culture is made up of core values and guiding principles. These core values and guiding principles are not fluid. They may shift from time to time, but usually in very incremental ways.

The culture of your organization is, in essence, how you, as a collective of people, treat each other inside the organization, how you as a collective treat those outside the organization, and how you as a collective conduct yourself in your work. It is the collective character and characteristics of the people in your organization. It also defines what impact you want to have as an organization.

Much has been written about the culture of organizations. In the management book *Good to Great,* Jim Collins' research says that what the culture of a company is doesn't matter; the great companies are intentional about their culture and stick with it.

All companies have a culture, whether intentional or not. Accidental or unintentional cultures tend to shift a lot depending on the leader and the people of the moment.

Most organizations have been very intentional about defining their culture. For startups, it's easy to just let things flow and let the culture develop as you grow. The challenge with this is that, without an intentional culture, you are like a stream without bedrock for your stream bed. You have a high risk of drying up or sinking below the surface and disappearing. Culture gives you the framework for decision making. We treat each other a certain way, so any behavior outside of that is not acceptable and not negotiable. It becomes automatic and helps you make the right decision. The culture also shapes how we treat customers or clients. It should also help shape the quality standards of how you make your products or deliver your services.

Culture is the bedrock that is the foundation of the organization. If it is the right culture, you can trace the success of the organization back to the culture. If you can't, then you may not have defined your culture as what it really is.

Once the culture is defined, the challenge is then living and working within that culture. Life happens. Pressures mount. A big customer demands something that can only be delivered by violating your culture. Your sales and/or your profit margins slip, and you know you can change that, but only by actions that violate your culture. What do you do?

Check your culture. It's okay to ask the question, "Is this part of our cultural foundation and unchangeable, or is it time to intentionally change the culture?" If it is foundational and unchangeable, then you must say no and deal with the consequences. If it is not, then make the change in an intentional way for the right reasons, not for the pressure of the moment, but for the long-term success of the business.

Enactus is a unique organization in many ways. It is a not-for-profit that relies on for-profit companies to fund it, as it prepares young leaders to be successful in business and in life. Our culture includes having a passion for our cause, which is very common among not-for-profits. However, because our cause is developing entrepreneurial leaders who take entrepreneurial action to improve lives, our culture also includes embracing competition, setting impact goals and working to achieve them. Many other not-for-profits, and even some of our business supporters, often asked, "Why do you have these students compete with each other instead of cooperating with each other?"

"Greater impact," was always my answer.

Every year I watched the national champions and world champions compete on stage and I would ask myself, "How will anyone ever top that?" Then the next year they, or usually their competitors, brought on new and better impact and would top the impact from the previous year. Part of our culture was knowing that competition leads to constant improvements, major breakthroughs, and striving for excellence. Competition helps us as humans always strive to be better.

Enactus launched a special competition with The Campbell Soup Company called "Let's Can Hunger." It had three parts:

- ⟡ creating awareness of hunger in America and the other countries engaged,
- ⟡ providing immediate relief through food drives, and
- ⟡ taking entrepreneurial action to help families break out of the hunger cycle by becoming employable, starting their own businesses, and by managing their financial resources more wisely.

To remind my team of the power of competition, I used a simple experiment tied to "Let's Can Hunger." To do our part at Enactus World HQ, we announced that we would join the food drive and asked all associates to bring canned food to the monthly meeting to be given to the local food banks. We were all good people. Well meaning. Charitable. Good-hearted. Every month for six months we brought in our canned food to the monthly meeting—if we remembered.

After six months I announced that we were going to have a competition by department to see who could bring in the most canned food. To make it fair, it was the most canned food per person in the department. The winners got to wear blue jeans every day for a month. The first month of the competition, the team brought in more cans of food than we had in the previous six months. By the end of the competition, we had provided our food bank with more food than any of us thought possible. It reinforced to my team why we built competition into "Let's Can Hunger." At the end of the year, the amount of food our students collected was amazing. More importantly, by the end of the three-year competition, over 10,000 families had been moved out of reliance on food banks.

USING COMPETITION TO ALWAYS SEEK THE BETTER WAY IS PART OF OUR CULTURE AND IT IS KEY TO OUR SUCCESS.

Culture is the bedrock of your organization, and it is shaped by and helps guide people. At its core, culture is about people. Getting the right people in your river is essential.

THE ENTERPRISE IS THE WATER

The water is that life form, that energy that brings everything else to life. At its core are the people in the enterprise. Regardless of the organization, companies, NGOs, or government agencies, they all start with the people in them. The founder starts the first drop of water flowing. As the water starts flowing, it now includes more people in the organization, customers, products, services and distributions systems.

PEOPLE MAKE THE DIFFERENCE

Recruiting, retaining, and inspiring people is the core of what an Accelerator Leader has to do. I deluded myself for years thinking that I would get the perfect team in place, only to be disappointed by people moving in and out of the team. The people in your organization will be fluid. How they are organized will also be fluid. People change and organizational charts change to fit the needs of the organization and the needs of the people. Don't build your team under the delusion that once in place the team is finished.

Don't build your organization under the delusion that if you find the perfect organizational chart it will be set forever (or even for a week). Several years ago, I had the opportunity to hear Irene Rosenfelt speak when she was the CEO of Kraft. She told us, "We have found that there is no perfect organization structure. There is only the best structure for what we need to do now." Only a few months later, the massive structure change splitting Kraft and creating Mondelez International was announced.

Build an organization knowing the river keeps flowing. Build it so that it continually attracts Accelerator Leaders and develops them into master guides and shepherds who inspire. Like a river, your talent ecosystem has to be built on the reality of fluidity.

PRODUCTS AND SERVICES ARE ALWAYS FLUID.

Are you a railroad or a transportation company? The question was asked by the book, *In Search of Excellence*, in 1982 and organizations still miss the point.

My question is, what is the impact your organization wants to have and how do you offer products and services to achieve that impact?

CUSTOMERS' NEEDS CHANGE.

The older I get, the more I sound like my grandfather ("When I was a kid . . .") It amazes me the products and services we can get every day that weren't available or didn't exist when I was a kid. I am able to work in a home office on a small farm in very rural Missouri, and I just talked to people in 10 countries. I can, at my fingertips, order and have anything I can think of delivered.

Customers change, products and services change. New products and innovative services change based upon the expectations of what customers need and want. You must stay fluid in what you offer and how you deliver it. Focus on the impact you want to have and offer the products and services that will accomplish that impact.

The impact doesn't change, but the things that allow you to achieve it does.

SUMMARY:

- ☞ Building a river means building an organization that is replicable, adaptable, scalable, and sustainable.
- ☞ All companies have a culture, whether intentional or not.
- ☞ Culture is about the people. Recruiting, retaining, and inspiring those people is the core of what an Accelerator Leader has to do.
- ☞ The impact doesn't change, but the things that allow you to achieve it does. Stay fluid.

ACTION STEPS:

⌐ Identify those parts of your organization that resemble a reservoir and those that resemble a river.

⌐ Identify those parts of your organization that are replicable, adaptable, and scalable.

⌐ Write a definition of your organization's culture.

⌐ Rate your organization from 1 to 10 (one being horrible and 10 being amazing) and its ability to recruit, retain, and inspire people.

⌐ Determine which actions you can take to improve your organization and people development.

CHAPTER FOURTEEN

BUILDING THE RIVER.

REPLICABLE

Itasca State Park in Minnesota is home of the headwaters of the Mississippi River. The water is 18 feet wide and knee deep. Every monster river has a headwater or starting point. All streams either start as a spring or are created from run-off from rain. Even the Nile started from a lake that was either from a spring or rain run-off—a drainage.

On my little farm, I have three streams. One is a run-off that began only a few hundred yards north of my farm. It runs well in wet weather but dries up during droughts. The second stream is fed by a combination of run-off and springs. The springs are a mile or two north of my farm. The run-off water comes from the ridge and fields to the north. There are two springs on my farm that add water to the flow. These springs keep small pockets of water in the stream even during severe droughts, assuring that the stream never dies. The third stream on my farm is fed by a nice spring that puts out water 24/7/365, even through droughts. All three streams converge at the south end of my property. It is inspiring to know my little farm is the headwater for one stream and is always sending water downstream to my neighbors, even in droughts.

From my farm, the combined streams flow to Spring Creek, then to Bear Creek, then into the Sac River, and then into the Osage River. From there it merges with the Missouri River that flows into the Mississippi River, ending in the Gulf of Mexico in New Orleans.

All organizations start from a spring or from rain. One or more people have a spark of an idea and out of it comes the spring that starts the enterprise rolling. Or, on the other hand, someone working in an existing organization wants to try something new and is told, "No, not here." Gravity pulls them away like the rain that falls and flows downstream until enough gathers to make a stream elsewhere.

When I met Jack Shewmaker and Sam Walton in 1984, Walmart was a large regional chain everyone knew would soon be national. I met Kemmons Wilson, the founder of Holiday Inn, in 1986. The Holiday Inn Company was a giant international hotel chain and Kemmons had already moved on to other ventures. Fortunately, Sam and Kemmons both took time to share their startup histories with me, and Jack became our chairman and my mentor as I stepped into the role of CEO of Enactus.

Kemmons started like a spring and Sam like a rain. Kemmons and his family took a cross-country vacation in the 1950s. They headed out and drove until they wanted to stop. Then they tried to find a hotel or motel to stay in. Today this sounds crazy, but back then that was how you had to do it. This was way before the internet and all the search sites. It was even before fax machines.

To get an advanced reservation, your choices were corresponding by mail or spending a lot of money on expensive long-distance calls, first to find a place and then to get a reservation on the dates you wanted. For Kemmons and most American families, the best choice was to show up and try their luck. Sometimes their luck paid off, and sometimes it didn't.

While Kemmons and his family found some motels that were gems, they often found substandard conditions at too high a price. On one such miserable trip, Kemmons came up with his spring of an idea. What American families wanted were safe, comfortable motels with consistent quality every time. They also needed a way to make reservations all along the trip in order to know where they were sleeping every night. Kemmons went to work designing the perfect motel for family cross-country road trips. The plan included big bright signs, appropriately sized rooms, swimming pools, and easy drive-up access to unload luggage and kids. Also needed was a family-priced restaurant that offered good, affordable food right there in the hotel. He named his establishment Holiday Inn after the hit movie from the 1940s in which the song "White Christmas" first debuted. Kemmons purposely designed his perfect prototype to be replicated. His vision was seeing Holiday Inns coast-to-coast across America.

Sam Walton was in an existing retail operation when he decided to start Walmart. After returning from World War II, he opened a Ben Franklin's Five and Dime in Rogers, Arkansas. It was so successful that, after a few years, his landlord refused to renew his lease so that a relative of the landlord could take over the store. Sam moved to Bentonville, Arkansas, and he opened a new Ben Franklin's Five and Dime on the town square. Today, it is now a museum about Walmart.

Sam was successful and added other Ben Franklin's franchises in a few other towns. Sam saw much more potential in rural Arkansas and rural America. He believed rural America was ready for a store that was all about discounts and had a much larger selection than the standard variety store. He took his idea to the leaders of the Ben Franklin's company. They did not see the opportunity. He could have used their distribution system and other expertise, but they were quite content with the status quo. Sam and his wife Helen went deep into debt to open the first Walmart in Rogers. For two years, Sam improved and perfected his store. He focused on understanding his customers' needs and wants. He implemented better purchasing systems and promotional programs. Sam built a replicable model that he knew would scale.

Enactus took off like a shooting star under its founder Sonny Davis. Unfortunately, the recession of 1982 hit like a hurricane. The support base at that time was large manufacturers and various oil companies. These were the very industries hit the hardest by the recession. As one of the major donors put it to Sonny, "I can't be sending workers out the back door with pink slips and give groups like you contributions, no matter how much good you're doing."

Because of this financial stress, Enactus was about to become another victim of the recession. The drop in resources led to a drop in universities being able to engage. As a result, Enactus dropped from over 100 colleges to 17 and from revenue of $400,000 per year to $30,000 with a matching $30,000 debt. As the faculty advisor for Southwest Baptist University (SBU), I attended the fall training workshop where Sonny shared the dire news, "If some person or organization doesn't step up to take over SIFE, we will have to shut down after this year."

I went back to my boss, the Chancellor of SBU, James Sells, and shared the news. I told him that I would like to take over Sonny's role. The university agreed to loan the money to clear the debt. (This was paid off in a few months.) They agreed to keep me and my assistant on their payroll if I also did some work for them. They provided us with office space, as well as access to the print shop, computer system, and other campus resources. Sonny approved of this arrangement and we began rebuilding Enactus on that campus. Without the rescue of SBU, Enactus would not exist today. It was two years later at SBU that Jack Shewmaker came to speak and became engaged.

My work was twofold—expand our donor base, and rebuild our program by adding new colleges. To grow the organization, I had to learn how to replicate the program to more campuses. My first step in rebuilding our program was to review my experience as a student and faculty advisor. Then I reached out to the faculty at the remaining 16 colleges to learn from them. What surprised me was how different each local program was. Membership ranged from big universities like Kent State and San Francisco State to small colleges like SBU and Harding College.

Enactus programs were located in different departments at different schools: accounting, economics, marketing, agriculture, and others. Their organization structures were also different. Some programs were extra-curricular clubs, some were co-curricular programs tied to some major, and some were actual classes. I began looking for the commonality and found some common threads. First, there were faculty advisors who believed in the mission of the organization. Second, there were administrations that gave them the academic freedom to engage. Third, there were academic competitions that reflected the mission of the organization.

Faculty chose to work with Enactus because they wanted to help students live better lives, not because they wanted to be seen as intellectual geniuses, even though many were brilliant academics. The key to replication was to use the competition process, including the judging criteria and recognition of the winners, to attract faculty who were committed to the mission. Size of school didn't matter. Geography didn't matter. Chapter structure didn't matter. Credit or no credit didn't matter. We allowed our local programs to be very entrepreneurial. We directed them to organize each program in the way that best fits its campus and community. We asked only that they focus the impact of their projects on our judging criteria that embody our mission. They focused on the judging criteria and organized themselves to maximize impact.

Once we understood our replication process, we were ready to scale.

One of the biggest challenges Sonny faced, and that I now faced, was that there was not a direct link to program and revenue growth. Universities that grow have increasing revenues, as do hospitals and many other non-profits. The Enactus model could never be built where an increase in program numbers was directly tied to an increase in revenue. We did learn that donors were more interested in supporting a growing organization and would give funds to help growth, but there was never a one-to-one match from growth to funding. This created a balancing act between program growth and revenue growth throughout my entire 30-year career. This dilemma required us to find a way to have a replicable method of raising revenue. The initial approach was for me to set a meeting with a prospective donor and tell our story and ask for money. I recruited about 1 in 10 prospects to be donors. Once they were donors, I asked them for a referral, which they usually gave, and then the process was repeated. This method did increase revenue but not very rapidly. We kept the doors open and grew a little, but it was a slow slog.

Recruiting Jack Shewmaker as chairman was a turning point in many ways. One of the most important of these was a change in our revenue recruiting model. In my first meeting with Jack, I asked him for a referral. He asked me what I would do with that referral. I told him I would ask them for support. "I won't do it," was Jack's reply.

Wow! I was decimated. My new chairman refused to give me any referrals. Now what?

"What got my attention and support was seeing the students," he continued. "What I will do is invite people to see and hear the students. After that, you can follow up however you want. You're a good fundraiser, and I mean no offense, but you'll never be able to sell the value of your organization as well as you would by letting people see the students' character and their good work," he explained.

Jack had just moved us from fundraisers to merchandisers. My ask became, "Please come and see the students." Jack invited top executives to come and see the students by being judges at the next competition. Once they saw the product of our students and their good work, they would become donors and inviters as well. We held breakfasts, lunches, and dinners where the primary draw was to hear Jack speak about the latest Walmart initiatives. Following Jack, we would have a team of students do a presentation about their projects. Jack soon got used to being upstaged by the quality of the students' programs and speaking abilities. Jack also shared the importance of gathering leaders together to give them time to get to know each other, establishing a network and a community. This also added value. As one donor put it, "I came because Jack invited me, but I stayed because of the students and the friends I made." Many other top executives followed Jack's example and gave our students a platform.

We now had a replicable model for program and revenue growth.

My favorite lunch spot is Crosstown Barbeque in Springfield, Missouri. I've been going there for lunch for over 25 years. I don't go every day, but I went there enough that you can order the "Alvin" special. Steve Williams is the owner. Kay has been the server there for 15 years. This is Steve's one and only restaurant. His success still comes from replication. When I go there, I go for two reasons. First is the food. I love barbeque and especially beef brisket. When I order the Alvin special, I know that every time I will get a large brisket sandwich, onion rings, and a diet Coke. I know it will be cooked to perfection and will have substantial amounts of brisket tucked between two layers of plain white bread.

For 15 years I ordered the large brisket sandwich with onion rings, only to be told by Kay that they don't serve onion rings. I told her to turn in the order anyway, and when it hit the kitchen I would hear a loud, "Hello, Alvin, how are you?" from Steve. Finally, one day I walked in and ordered my usual, but there was no push back from Kay and no loud hello from Steve. Instead, Steve brought my order to me, complete with onion rings. "You win," Steve said, "I now offer onion rings."

The Alvin special was born.

The second reason I eat at Crosstown Barbeque is the people: Steve and Kay. If I go in and one or both of them are not in that day, it's not quite the same. The food is good, but the experience isn't as rich. I often time my lunch so I can get there at the end of the rush, so Steve will have time to come out and sit with me and catch up on family news. Steve has built Crosstown's success on replication—with each experience, you know you will enjoy quality food and Steve's incredible hospitality. Steve has no interest in scaling beyond one restaurant, in part because he knows that he is part of the secret sauce, and in part because he measures his success and impact on the number of friends he's made. For him, scaling to more places would get in the way of getting to know people deeply.

Once you have developed or discovered your replicable model, you have to decide how much you want to scale that model. This comes back to the question of how much and what type of impact you want to have. Sam and Kemmons decided on large scale. Steve Williams chose a smaller scale to make deeper connections to his customers. Whatever you choose is okay. Just be sure it's a conscious choice. Do not settle for less.

SCALABLE: SPRING TO STREAM TO RIVER TO THE MIGHTY MISSISSIPPI.

Once you know how a stream grows, you know how to make it scale. Streams grow as they flow downstream. They increase in size by hitting new springs and by having water drain into them from rain and snow melts, but the big growth comes when they merge with another stream. **To accelerate your organization, you need to decide what scale you want to achieve the impact you desire.**

Once Kemmons Wilson got his Holiday Inn prototype perfected, he was ready to scale. He had a great concept, but now he needed the capital to scale it. Kemmons decided to use the franchising system to grow. This allowed him to have others bring in their capital and have skin in the game. The franchise model also gave Kemmons the ability to control the perfected model and deliver on customer expectations. Holiday Inns, Inc. would make money from franchise fees and selling franchise branded supplies to the franchisees as well as owning some of their own motels.

To add value to this model and bring even more scale, Kemmons added the Holidex system. Holidex used the hot new technology of Telex. It allowed a customer to go to any Holiday Inn in any town, including one's hometown, and get a reservation for every night of a trip in any Holiday Inn across the country. Revolutionary! Kemmons' brainchild of Holiday Inns occurred when President Eisenhower built the interstate highway system to enable us to move troops quickly from coast to coast in case of war. Fortunately, we have never had to use these interstate highways for this reason. Instead, the interstate highway system became the new river system for America. Coupled with the rapid increase in new and more reliable cars, it made America a country on the move. It also resulted in many brand-new highway interchanges that were the perfect places to build Holiday Inns.

Kemmons and his franchise partners dropped a Holiday Inn at almost every interstate exit across the country.

For Sam Walton it was about helping people save money so they could live better. Sam lived in rural America and knew it well. He realized that, compared to people living in cities, his rural friends and neighbors were spending more and had fewer choices. He knew that if he changed the retail process he could help people save money and live better.

The success of Walmart is documented well in the museum on the square in Bentonville, and it is explained in detail in Mr. Walton's autobiography, *Made in America*. I learned it firsthand from Jack Shewmaker. Sam didn't just open a bigger store—he built a logistics system powered by technology that filled stores in rural America with an amazing array of product choices at prices as good as, or better than, those in the big cities.

The model for scaling was to build a distribution center that could serve 150 stores. Build the stores around it to capacity and then move up the road and build another distribution center and build stores around it. Walmart, in essence, built its own river system that connected distribution centers to stores. Each new distribution center was like drilling a well or finding a spring. It created a new stream. Walmart also changed retailing in a major way by introducing Jack Shewmaker's concept of everyday low pricing. Jack and I grew up in a retail environment where retailers tricked customers into shopping. Bait and switch was an acceptable practice, as was the perpetual clearance or going-out-of-business sale and the dominant end-of-the-month major markdowns.

What retailers didn't understand was that they were merely training customers to wait to buy when there were markdowns. I remember asking my mother once what it meant to be rich. She said it was, "being able to go to the store any day of the week and buy whatever I need." Jack

Shewmaker firmly believed the Walmart brand should be about everyday low prices (EDLP) that would build customers' loyalty. He also knew that EDLP required EDLC (everyday low cost). Walmart built its logistics system to fulfill the promise of EDLP through EDLC.

The interstate highway system was a new river system that helped Kemmons Wilson scale his Holiday Inns. In rural America, there was the push for farm-to-market roads. As farmers began using trucks instead of horse-drawn wagons to get to and from town, it became important for them to have good, safe roads. My state of Missouri very proudly started the farm-to-market paved road system in the 1960s, and it was great for farmers. It also meant that farmers could travel much farther to larger markets to buy and sell their goods.

The unintended consequence of paved highways was that farmers drove past their small towns to the bigger cities. When I was growing up, my family lived halfway between Bolivar, Missouri (population 6,000) and Springfield, Missouri (population 100,000). Over 70% of our trips to town were to Springfield until Walmart store number 46 opened in Bolivar. We now had a reason to go to Bolivar, knowing that most of what we needed was at Walmart. From my perspective, Walmart brought a lot of commerce back to small towns before it moved into cities as well.

Scale is one of those things that often changes as it grows. Sam Walton started with a vision of stores in small towns that would grow into stores in small cities. This grew into stores in every state and cities large and small and then into other countries, all in Sam's lifetime. Kemmons' vision was Holiday Inns for families' cross-country vacations. The vision then became building a giant global hotel chain, which was accomplished in his lifetime as well.

When I stepped in as CEO of Enactus in 1982, we had 16 colleges. In 1983 we had 16 colleges, and in 1984 we grew to an amazing 22 colleges. I would like to tell you that it was because I was perfecting the model that we didn't grow very fast. But in reality it was because we needed a new stream, a new river, and that came with the connection to Jack Shewmaker and Walmart. Jack became chairman in 1984, and in 1985 we had 72 colleges, growth of more than 300% in one year. We moved from little creek to small river overnight.

Jack's and Walmart's support sent the message to colleges and donors that we were a valuable organization doing good work that could be trusted. I knew that the key to our replication and scaling was recruiting the right faculty advisors, so my proposal to Walmart was to fund a stipend to reward every faculty advisor who brought a team to competition and to honor those faculty members by naming them Walmart/Sam's Club Free Enterprise Fellows. This financial reward and honor were the core of our marketing efforts to faculty. They received an invitation from Jack Shewmaker, the vice-chairman of Walmart, asking them to become Walmart/Sam's Club Fellows and offering them a $1,000 stipend at the end of the year. This exploded our program numbers, and we experienced double-digit growth. The honor was made even more significant after Mr. Walton's death when his family agreed to let us change the name to Sam M. Walton Free Enterprise Fellows, a designation the faculty members still carry.

While Kemmons, Sam, and I all used different approaches to scale our organizations, the common denominator was people. Kemmons built a team around him and a network of franchisees that delivered the scale. It was people who bought the land and built the motels. It was people who marketed those motels to America, and it was people who delivered on the promise of friendly service and clean rooms. If you read *Made in America,* you will see that Sam Walton chose to tell the story of Walmart's success through the people. These people included those who helped him learn retailing at his Ben Franklin's stores, and then those like Jack Shewmaker, David Glass, Don Soderquist, and others who are Walmart's pioneers. He also talked about his associates in the stores and his customers who he knew were his true bosses.

Scaling requires the right systems and processes, but most importantly, scaling requires the right people. At our core, Enactus scaled because of the faculty and key people on that early leadership team that served the faculty and donors: Sidney Lilly, Mark Holmes, Fritz Teller, Carolyn Savoy, and the many great people who followed.

Don't let the replicable and scalable model become a reservoir. Building a replicable model can lead to significant scaling of that model, but it may not lead to maximum impact and scale. My observations and experience tell me that the difference is whether or not the replicable, scalable model also includes adaptability. The temptation of a replicable, scalable model is that you focus so much on your current model that you turn it into a reservoir. You build so many systems and processes that preserving your model becomes your goal, rather than maximizing your impact. The "we are railroads" syndrome sets in and then eventually the dam breaks.

ADAPTABLE: DON'T FIGHT GRAVITY

Replicability and adaptability seem to be at odds, but they are not. At their headwaters, streams start out with a mineral content and ecosystem of fish and other creatures. As the water moves downstream and experiences different soils and joins with other streams, the mineral content and the various species in its ecosystem change. It is replicable as new streams start out one of the same two ways, spring or drainage, but inherent in their replicable model is the ability to adapt. Streams function under one truth: gravity. Gravity is always present. Gravity will always pull water to a lower elevation. Water's natural flow is to always follow the pull of gravity. This requires the rivers to bend and twist to follow gravity to the next lower elevation. Gravity requires rivers to be adaptable. Rivers survive by following gravity, not fighting it.

Earlier I made the case for building a river and not a reservoir, because life is fluid. Even the very land we stand on is only an illusion of solidarity. The most fluid things in nature are people. The very intellect and soul that separates us from the animals makes us more fluid. We change our minds; we are highly mobile; we progress out of our own efforts; we are fickle. Organizations are built on the collective actions of people and will, therefore, always be subject to gravity. The difference is that our gravity is the reality of change. Water in rivers can't stop gravity, and people in organizations can't stop change.

EVERY REPLICABLE, SCALABLE MODEL MUST ALSO BE ADAPTABLE TO REACH MAX- IMUM IMPACT AND BE SUSTAINABLE.

Walmart had an excellent replicable scalable model, but Sam and its leaders knew that they also had to be adaptable to better serve their growing number of customers and to fend off their growing competition. Even under their original model, they were very adaptable. I learned early that real estate meetings at Walmart were nearly sacred. You did not ask anyone to attend an event that conflicted with real estate meeting dates. At first, I didn't get it. I thought, "It's just real estate." Then I came to understand that it was about where they located stores and where they replaced old stores with new stores.

Historically, retail was all about the buildings. You built a store, and that was not only where you were, it was also who you were. Walmart was about the customer and wanted its stores located where they could best serve their customers. They built their store construction and financing model around being able to relocate stores to better sites within the same towns to accommodate customers' changing travel and shopping patterns. Real estate meetings were designed to let a large group of leaders weigh in on where to build new stores and where to relocate existing stores if necessary. If you missed the meeting, you had no voice, so you did not miss the real estate meeting.

Giant big-city department stores and small-town stores around the center square died off because they built their model based on their buildings, not based on customer needs. Walmart, at its core, has been a technology company. That has helped them stay adaptable. Sam and his leadership team used airplanes to visit stores and potential new locations. Walmart installed one of the first satellite systems to record store data in real time. Jack Shewmaker, when president of Walmart, was co-chair of the task force that created the standards for bar coding. Different industries and companies were using different bar code methods. Mr. Walton and Jack Shewmaker saw the value of how those little bars on the side of boxes would empower the use of computers and technology, revolutionizing logistics and retailing. They took a lead in creating a standard and mandated it for their vendors. By the time I met Jack Shewmaker and Sam Walton in 1984, Walmart was the second most powerful computing power in America, second only to the Pentagon.

This technology lead gave Walmart the ability to expand beyond general merchandise to grocery, and from one retail format to many, eventually expanding to other countries. The products and services they offer have expanded rapidly and changed often in order to meet consumer demand. Their impact isn't any particular product; it is "Save Money. Live Better."

This adaptability and use of technology was not always easy to do. Jack Shewmaker was fond of telling the story of how Sam Walton fired him not just once, but three times, all in the same day. Jack, as president, had been working on the purchase of a satellite system for the headquarters and all the stores. Sam was on a trip and Jack asked him if he could get a green light. Sam said yes. When Sam got back from his trip, he saw the details of the agreement, including the 50-million-dollar price tag.

He walked into Jack's office and said, "You didn't tell me the cost was 50 million dollars. You're fired!"

Jack got up and walked out to the parking lot and got into his truck. Sam followed him and spoke to Jack through his truck's window. "Are you sure this is all worth 50 million?" Sam asked.

"It will revolutionize how we supply our stores and will give us a giant leap over our competition."

"Okay," Sam said, "Let's go inside and talk about it."

They went back to Sam's office where Sam looked at the price tag again and said, "Jack, this is more money than we have the authority to spend without board approval."

"I know," said Jack.

"You're fired!" yelled Sam.

Jack went to his office and started to clear out his things. A few minutes later Sam walked into Jack's office and asked again, "Are you sure this is best for the company?"

"Yes," was the reply.

"Put your things back. You're not fired," Sam responded and returned to his office.

Fifteen minutes later, Sam walked back to Jack's and asked, "Why didn't you tell me this would cost $50,000,000?"

"Because I knew you would say no," was Jack's response.

"You are fired!" This appeared to be Sam's final decision. Jack packed his things in a box and walked down the hall on his way out.

Sam then yelled from his desk, "Jack, wait!" and stepped into the hall. "Did you think signing this contract would cost you your job?" he asked.

Jack replied, "I knew that signing this contract was in the best interest of the company's long-term success. I decided that by signing it, you and the company were committed to it, and that if that cost me my job, I had still done my best to serve you and the company."

"If you believe in this that much, then unpack your things and get back to work. We have to sell a lot of goods to pay that 50 million," was Sam's final response.

When Jack Shewmaker retired from Walmart, Enactus hosted a retirement dinner for him. Sam agreed to cosign the invitation with me to the dinner. It was a great honor to have Sam Walton cosign an invitation with me. At the dinner, to Jack's surprise, we announced the construction of our own headquarters building. The name of the building would be The Jack Shewmaker National Headquarters. A few days later I got a call from Jack. He said, "I was very surprised that you announced a new building without me knowing about it since I'm still on your board. I'm also upset that you didn't get my approval before announcing you were going to use my name."

"Jack, I'm sorry to surprise you," I said, "but it's not like I signed a 50-million-dollar contract." There was a pause, and then Jack said, "I never should have told you that story. I am very honored. Just make sure you ask the next time."

Though it was a technology company that provided customers merchandise selection and value, Walmart did not recognize the power of the internet early enough. If they had, Amazon might not exist today. Walmart is by far the world's largest technology-driven merchant, they are playing catch up to Amazon in online sales. It's a race I believe Walmart will win.

At his first shareholders meeting, Doug McMillon, the current CEO of Walmart, made a comment that was transformational, but not all of the 20,000 attendees got it. Past CEOs, including Sam Walton, had always said, "When asked how we run a company so large, our answer is always, we run Walmart one store at a time."

Doug said, "When asked how we run Walmart our answer is: We will run Walmart one customer at a time. We will deliver to her what she wants, where she wants it, and when she wants it." Game on!

Walmart, at its core, is still about "Save Money. Live Better." It's delivered through technology powered by great people doing extraordinary things.

Holiday Inns' perfect model was soon replicated. As Kemmons told me, "We spent lots of money doing due diligence to pick the right locations. Our competition didn't spend a penny on due diligence. They just built a motel right beside us or just across the intersection." The next big thing for Holiday Inns was the Holidome, which was an indoor pool attached to each Holiday Inn. That, too, was soon replicated by the competition.

As business travel and family vacation budgets increased, travel needs and wants also changed. Holiday Inns built several new formats to meet those needs. When the board decided they should move into the casino business, Kemmons didn't agree. He didn't think it was consistent with their family brand. The board voted for casinos and Kemmons resigned from the board.

Because of the speed of change in their industry, Holiday Inns was challenged to adapt rapidly. They are still a viable company but are no longer the dominant player they once were.

The entire hospitality industry is facing its biggest challenge in decades. The largest lodging company doesn't even own one hotel. Airbnb and its new rivals are arguably the ultimate river in this industry.

Because I have been connected to so many companies in so many industries, I've seen many transitions in my 30-year career.

Enactus' scalability was tied to being adaptable. When I was a student and faculty advisor, the judging criterion was, "How creative and innovative were the students at promoting free enterprise?" This criterion was tied to our mission of improving lives through free enterprise, but as CEO I soon learned it was a barrier to growth in the academic market. Our current and prospective faculty told us, "We don't promote anything. We teach and educate."

The criterion was changed to, "How creative and innovative were the students at teaching the principles of free enterprise?" Under this criterion, we had hundreds of students teaching thousands of students in classrooms. As the organization grew, we continued to evolve but stayed true to our core mission. We noticed that more and more of our college teams were going outside of the classroom and teaching students through hands-on business simulations, such as mock cities, or by running actual businesses, such as making candy and selling it during recess.

We also noticed more and more college teams funding their education projects by running a business of their own, such as a snack bar, coffee shop, or souvenir shop on campus. We also noticed that the competition judges, who were business owners or executives, rewarded these teams by giving them the wins at competition. Soon every team was following the winners. We adjusted the criteria to reflect not only teaching the principles of free enterprise, but helping people understand how market economies and businesses work. As one Board member put it, "If you want more people to believe in capitalism, create more capitalists."

On a fishing trip, Jack Shewmaker, Jack Kahl, myself, and several others got into one of those over-the-campfire conversations. Jack Shewmaker began, "I don't get why other people don't believe in free enterprise the way we here all do. Alvin, what is the biggest reason those opposed to free enterprise use to attack it?"

My response was, "We all know that to succeed, free enterprise has to be dynamic, and there are always winners but also some losers. We all know people who have fallen through the cracks in the economy and don't prosper from free enterprise. These cracks in the system are what the critics use to call for more welfare. They are the basis of Karl Marx's socialist and communist arguments."

Jack Kahl asked, "How do we change that?"

"By getting our students to go directly to those being left out and helping them become part of the system. It doesn't do any good to teach people how free enterprise works if they don't ever see themselves as being a part of the system," was Shewmaker's reaction.

We began a special competition called Success 2000 that rewarded teams who helped others become active participants in free enterprise by helping them start micro businesses, increase their education, get jobs, and manage their money better. The effect was that thousands of people were moved from reliance on government assistance to self-reliance, and thousands of new small businesses were formed. It was called Success 2000 because we used the year 2000 as the goal date to report our total results. Once the year 2000 rolled in, we decided that, instead of a new name for this special effort, we would merge it into our overall program and adjusted the judging criteria accordingly. The evolution of the organization continued, but we stayed true to our core, helping people live better lives through free enterprise.

The biggest adjustment to Enactus came when the Soviet Union collapsed. There were millions of people in the former Soviet Union who were now living in economies transitioning from command communist government-controlled economies to market economies. They were all asking the same question *Mikhail Gorbachev* had asked Len Roberts decades before, "How does this thing called a market economy work?"

Many of our Sam Walton Fellows in America were being asked by their universities to travel to these countries and share the answer. Many of the faculty from universities in these countries were coming to America in exchange programs to learn for themselves so they could teach their own people.

Robin Anderson was the Sam Walton Fellow at the University of Nebraska Lincoln—Big Red—and ran the entrepreneurship program. Under a *United States Agency for International Development (USAID)* grant, he travelled to Central Asia and brought back faculty to study entrepreneurship and market economics at Nebraska. Many of them joined the Enactus Team while there and became very engaged with the program. When they returned to their countries (Kazakhstan, Uzbekistan, Kyrgyzstan, Tajikistan, and others), they began Enactus teams on their home campuses.

A year later I got a call from Robin. He asked if they could do a competition in Central Asia. I said "of course." I travelled with Robin to Kazakhstan and then Kyrgyzstan to attend the first Enactus competition outside of the USA. The winning team of this multi-country competition got to compete at the SIFE International Exposition in Kansas City. This was a very cosmetic name change to what had been for years the SIFE National Exposition, where only American teams competed. The Central Asia champion now had to compete with over 150 USA Schools for the title of International Champion.

Once the word got out about this first competition outside the USA, we were flooded by USA Sam Walton Fellows who had relationships and exchange programs around the world. They had people who wanted to be in Enactus. Most of them were given the green light. They were encouraged to go plant our flag at any university in any country where they had a connection.

Our replication model was designed to build teams at universities. This enabled our USA-based faculty to translate our model and our materials into other languages and to start new teams on campuses. We even offered to pay the same stipend level of $1,000 a year to the faculty. At first, this worked well and got us started at one or two universities in several countries. Dr. Robin Anderson agreed to lead this effort part-time, and the University of Nebraska let him include it in his duties for the entrepreneurship school.

Trouble soon began. The second competition in Central Asia did not go so well. The team from the host country won. The teams from the other countries noticed that there were more judges from that country than their countries, so they protested the results, claiming judge bias. Several of the universities said they would drop out if they had to compete in another country. They wanted their own national competition. Additionally, we discovered that a $1,000 stipend, which was a nice thank you in the USA, was equivalent to 2-3 months' pay in Central Asia. We had faculty on campuses fighting over being the Enactus advisor, not because they believed in our mission, but because they wanted the $1,000. We didn't get faculty who were passionate about our work, but rather those who had the highest rank.

Eventually reality set in. We couldn't build an international organization working directly with university campuses, which was our core competency. Instead, we now needed to build national organizations that would work with universities and in-country donors. We also learned that we could not fund universities and faculty stipends in other countries at the same rate as we did in the USA. We needed to be very adaptable about how we established organizations in each country and about how that national organization interfaced with universities. We needed a whole new replication model but had little time to develop it.

We learned early that the key to our success in every country would be recruiting the right country leader and the right board chair. The country leader was the staff person who was devoted, usually full time, to Enactus. The board chair was the volunteer leader of the board whose main responsibility was to mentor the Enactus Country Leader and invite other business leaders to see the students in action. The board chair would then help the Country Leader recruit these other business leaders to become donors and eventually board members. Where and how could we find the right people? We needed master guides.

KPMG and Rich Products came to the rescue— Tom Moser and Bob Rich, to be more precise. Above, I explained how Tom became the chairman of Enactus and launched the first World Cup. He and KPMG did much more. KPMG was in over 150 countries where they were connected to many businesses that were their clients. They were also connected to all the top universities, where they recruited their top talent. Bob Rich, my master fishing guide, followed Tom as chair of Enactus and also jumped into our international expansion, connecting us in all the countries where Rich Products operated.

Tom recruited KPMG senior partners to volunteer as country board chairs to recruit country leaders and hold their national competitions in KPMG offices. Bob did the same at Rich Products. In addition, KPMG and Rich

Products provided financial support to country operations. Enactus' global expansion was made possible only because KPMG and Rich Products were willing to be our master guides.

WHEN ENTERING NEW COUNTRIES, NEW INDUSTRIES, NEW WATERS, NEW SPACES OF ANY KIND, FIND THE MASTER GUIDE AND THEN LISTEN TO THAT GUIDE.

Scaling internationally and adapting to different cultures required a new capacity of the Enactus staff. After the success of the first Enactus World Cup, Chairman Tom Moser made it very clear that Enactus had to ramp up staffing and move from part-time to full-time leadership for the international division. Dr. Robin Anderson did not want to leave his University position, so we needed to make a change. Peter Drucker, the ultimate business leadership guru, has said, "You don't put your best people on your biggest problem, you put them on your biggest opportunity." The answer for us was pretty clear.

Bruce Nasby, our Sr. VP of Development, had been very successful for us and was our best talent. Going international was our biggest opportunity. Bruce jumped in with both feet. He was given almost unbelievable goals by Tom Moser, and he delivered 100% on nearly every one of them. We also knew that we needed to add regional leadership capable of organizing country operations and interfacing with our global donors like KPMG. One of our two best hires for this was Sylvester John, a native of Sierra Leone educated in Ghana who had just graduated from North Florida University. He had been part of the movement to bring Enactus to Afghanistan.

Our other best hire, Yusef Majiduv, who had also been part of the Afghanistan plans, was one of the first people to help Robin Anderson in Central Asia. The Central Asia country operations were struggling to raise money. Yusef told me that there wasn't much private money there because charitable giving was not part of the culture. The only donations they could get were in-kind donations of office space and event expenses, such as competition rooms, student sleeping rooms, and meals.

No one was willing to make cash contributions to fund a full-time staff, travel, or any of the other things required to run a national organization.

I travelled to the region and visited Baku, the capital of Azerbaijan. The food there is amazing, surpassed only by the incredible hospitality. On the way to one of our meetings, we drove down a street that had a Mercedes and Ferrari dealership, as well as a store for every major fashion brand. As we drove down what looked like Rodeo Drive in Beverly Hills, I asked Yusef, "If there is little private money in the region, who is buying all these high dollar cars and clothes?"

"There are some very wealthy people, but they are not very charitable," he replied.

"Yusef, why do these people buy these cars and these clothes at these very high prices? Is it because these things are really that much better than the moderately priced things?" I asked.

"They buy these cars and high fashions so people will know how successful they are. They do it to boost their egos," was his answer.

"That's great," I replied, "Now you have your answer to fundraising. If you can't appeal to their charitable nature, appeal to their egos. When they give you money, thank them very publicly. Make them heroes on stage in front of the thousands of students they are supporting. Get them all the press possible so their peers will want the same fame."

Within a year, this approach had changed their financial success. It only took making one successful entrepreneur locally famous to get others to sign up. Adapting the fundraising appeal worked.

One of my favorite Master Guides is Juan Servitje, one of the top business leaders in Mexico, and this is the story why. Because we thought we knew everything about how to do Enactus, we launched in Mexico doing everything the same way we did it in the United States. We recruited donors in Mexico to support the organization, but then we (mostly I) proceeded to tell them how to run everything our way. Due to this approach and other missteps, we encountered years of struggles.

The biggest challenge was finding the right person to lead the country operation. The local donors did not want to commit to spending the money necessary to attract a truly qualified candidate, so instead they settled on a modest budget and a person they could afford.

In each case, the individual lacked the skills to raise the money needed to run the operation, so they would leave and be replaced by a new leader who also was not up to the task. As the chicken and egg cycle continued, many of the original donors left out of frustration. This situation lasted for a few years and we were at the point of deciding to either pull out of Mexico or give it one more try by hiring at the right level.

As I mentioned Juan is one of the top business leaders in Mexico. When we established Enactus in Mexico, Juan was invited by Bob Rich to consider helping Enactus get started. Juan was the President & CEO of Rich Products for Latin-America as a result from partnering with Rich. He liked the value proposition Enactus had for the students, communities and countries and agreed to help.

Juan is a person I would describe as smooth as silk but as tough as leather. He is always the consummate gentleman even when he has to deliver a tough message. I met with Juan in one of my visits to Mexico. In this case, his comments were very pointed but delivered as kindly as possible. "The core values, mission and competition procedures of the organization are universal and should be applied the same in every country," Juan explained. "But you need to realize that there are many things about how the organization must operate in each country that are different than how things need to be done in the United States." Juan went on to explain that one reason the donors in Mexico were reluctant to give enough to fund the right country leader was that we were not listening well enough to them about these differences. Therefore, we were making the wrong hiring decisions.

Juan knew that the Enactus country leaders needed to be CEO capable and CEO compatible. That meant he or she had to be able to act like a CEO and execute and fundraise like a CEO. Additionally, this person had to be able to relate to the top CEOs in the country in the way they conducted themselves, communicated, and executed their work. Many of the former leaders we tried in Mexico came from academia and were great in a classroom but couldn't make the transition to the boardroom. Juan pointed out that the type of leader who could relate well with CEOs and business owners in the Mexican culture had a slightly different style and skill set than a business leader in the United States. I agreed to engage the Mexico donors more in recruiting the Enactus Mexico country leader, and the Enactus global board agreed to give it one more try due to Juan's commitment. The board also agreed to underwrite the increased cost for hiring the right level of leader if he or she could not raise the full support in the first year.

Thanks to Juan's persistence we were ready to collaborate with the Mexico Board and find the right leader. We agreed on hiring Jesus Esparza. He had great integrity and appeared to have the right intellect and abilities to be CEO and CEO compatible.

The situation at this point was more difficult than what we imagined. Jesus inherited an organization that had been losing credibility with past donors and universities due to our wrong decisions from the previous years, so when Jesus knocked on their doors again he found them closed. At that time Enactus Mexico was 12 Universities and 2 in-country donors. To make things worse, Juan faced a serious health situation that forced him to disconnect from everything not just Enactus.

After a tough first semester we had the first great opportunity. The CEO of one of the world's largest companies was coming to Mexico City. He was a friend of Enactus, and I convinced him to attend an Enactus event. We had a short time, so I called Jesus to tell him the good but challenging news. He needed to put together an event and invite on very short notice the top business leaders in Mexico to attend. The event went well with a dozen top executives attending a very exclusive breakfast, but Jesus was seen by the CEO's local team as an intruder. When I called the CEO about how the event went, he said, "My team in Mexico doesn't think your country leader in Mexico is the right person. You should consider making a change if you want their continued support."

Ouch! I was needing to make a decision. But this time I was confident we had hired the right talent. I knew that all Jesus was needing was a mentor, so a few days later during a 1:1 meeting with Jesus I shared with him the role the chairman of Enactus World Wide had in my life, and how he mentored me. Jesus captured immediately the idea. Later that year Jesus informed me that Juan agreed to rejoin the board in Mexico. Juan had recovered his health and one of the first things he was reconnecting with was Enactus. According to several studies, having a purpose in life creates meaning and improves health, I'm convinced that this is 100% true with Juan. He is not just a business leader, but someone that leads with purpose.

The following year Juan became the chairman at Enactus Mexico and Jesus' mentor. This duo became one of the most successful teams I ever seen in the world. He took Jesus under his wing and taught him the why of strategic planning, tight execution, how to build strong relationships with top CEOs and to always, always keep your integrity. Juan took the initiative to introduce Jesus and Enactus to many top CEOs in Mexico and beyond. Juan encouraged Jesus to add to his education by participating in Stanford University's Executive Education programs.

One of the most strategic initiatives Juan has led is to build a national board with elite business and social leaders that embraced Enactus' purpose. This group includes women and men from the top national and international corporations, Mexico's education officers and recognized leaders. Once again, Juan was guiding me about how Enactus was providing global guidelines, but success was only achievable by acting locally.

In 2013, we intended to hold the Enactus World Cup in China but the government approval was going to take much longer than time allowed. We had to find a country program on short notice that would step up and help us and also help its own operation. Mexico, Juan, and Jesus came to the rescue. We found a great venue in Cancun. Juan reminded me that while this was an Enactus Global event, we needed to make several adjustments to attract the top leaders of Mexico. This time I listened. Juan and Jesus delivered. The top business leaders of Mexico stepped up to attend and bring their friends. It was one of the most attended, and financially successful Enactus World Cups.

The dress code for the final dinner for VIPs included wearing the traditional Mexican dress shirt "Guayabera". Juan gave me one as his gift. Five of Mexico's billionaires and dozens of top CEOs attended, and it was very clear that they all liked and respected Jesus. Because of Juan, Jesus had not only become CEO capable and compatible, but had moved up to being billionaire compatible.

Soon after, Jesus was awarded a significant grant from a large corporation to develop a leadership training program for the leaders of all the non-profits receiving awards from the company's foundation. That grant was provided by the same company whose CEO wasn't sure Jesus was the right fit to be the leader in Mexico—the ultimate proof of what a Master Guide can do.

As I'm writing these lines, Enactus Mexico has become of the the largest and more efficient operation at the Enactus country operations network with almost 500 universities in the program, and one of the top leadership & entrepreneurship organizations in Latin America.

SUMMARY:

- ✎ All organizations start from an idea, like a spring or rain.
- ✎ What do you want your organization to look like? How do you replicate that?
- ✎ To accelerate your organization, you need to decide what scale you want to achieve the impact you desire.

⇗ Scaling requires the right systems and processes, but most of all, the right people.

⇗ Each replicable, scalable model must also be adaptable to be sustainable and achieve maximum impact.

⇗ When entering new spaces of any kind, find the master guide and listen to them.

ACTION STEPS:

⇗ Determine the origins of your organization. Was it a spring or rain? Who were the founders and what was their desired impact?

⇗ Evaluate how your organization has continued that impact or how they changed their desired impact.

⇗ Visualize the scale your organization needs to achieve the impact desired.

⇗ Analyze the systems and processes of your organization and determine which ones help foster the flow of the river and which ones appear to be building dams.

⇗ Having identified what your organization does that is replicable and scalable in the previous chapter, evaluate how they can also be adaptable to achieve maximum impact.

⇗ Identify the master guides who will take you to your next new stream.

CHAPTER FIFTEEN

BUILD MOMENTUM.

One day, back on my childhood farm, a bunch of us were heading out to feed the animals across the creek. It had been raining all night, but not much more than a normal spring rain. We were surprised to see that the creek had risen so much. It was about a foot higher than usual at the crossing. The water was running a bit fast and it was over a half-mile walk to the bridge. My buddy Ralph and I decided to man up, at the age of thirteen, and cross the creek. After all, it was only a foot deeper.

As soon as we stepped in, we were goners. The water may have only been a foot deeper than normal, but what we didn't know was that the bottom of the creek had washed out by three feet. We stepped into a big hole of water. We were up to our necks and, in milliseconds, we were being swept down the creek, choking and gasping for air.

I was lucky; the current pushed me into the bank we had started from. The other guys grabbed me and pulled me out. Ralph was not so lucky. The current pushed him to the other side of the creek and began to push him downstream. He was going faster than the guys could keep up. They yelled, "Grab that tree in front of you and hold on!"

Ralph did, and his motion stopped. The rain had stopped, and the creek had crested, so Ralph would be okay as long as he held on to that tree. One of the guys ran back to the barn and brought back some ropes. We threw one to Ralph. He put it around himself. We told him to jump off the tree so we could pull him to our side.

"Are you nuts!?" Ralph yelled. "You're not going to drag me back through that water, now or ever. Three of you will walk your sorry rear ends down to the bridge. Cross the bridge and walk back here to me. Then you'll use the rope to pull me up the bank and out of this creek. Then I will walk back across the bridge. Is that clear?" That was not the voice I recognized of meek and mild thirteen-year-old Ralph. He had truly manned up. "Yes, sir!" we all simultaneously replied. In an hour we were back home in dry clothes. Ralph was the new leader.

That day I learned a valuable lesson about momentum. I will never forget the power of that wall of water as it hit me and drove me downstream. I have since learned that water flowing at 7 MPH has the equivalent pressure of air moving at EF 5 tornado wind speed. Water moving at 25 MPH has the same pressure as winds moving at 790 MPH; faster than the speed of sound.

That is momentum. We witness the power and speed of momentum swings more in sports than perhaps other parts of life. As a fan of the Kansas City Chiefs, I've grown accustomed to seeing big positive momentum in the beginning of a game or season, only to see the momentum disappear in the fourth quarter or the playoffs. I got to see the Chiefs play in a Super Bowl with my father. I hope I will get to see the Chiefs play in a Super Bowl with my kids. Once in a generation. Is that too much to ask? Andy and Patrick, this is our year!

Accelerator Leaders create momentum. The momentum of a river is created by gravity, the pitch or slope of the bedrock, and the amount of flow being pushed between the banks. Narrow rivers in steep mountains run much faster than wide rivers in flat terrain. Did you know that the Florida Everglades is a river? It is so wide and moves so slowly over the flat Florida peninsula that it is choked with vegetation which has taken root in its bed. It looks and acts like a swamp, but it's a river.

Building a river and maximizing the impact of that river requires building momentum. It has been a privilege for me to partner with and connect to so many great companies in my career. Observing so many companies and nonprofit organizations over the years, I've come to the conclusion that leadership does matter and the CEO or top leader of an organization makes all the difference in the momentum of an organization. In Jim Collins' *Good to Great* he told his researchers at the beginning that he didn't want the success of the companies to come down to "it's all about the CEO." But then when the research was concluded, it showed that it was truly the CEO that drove the company's success. When I read this, I laughed out loud in agreement. My conclusion from real world observation was now backed up by research data.

While I know that the Accelerator Leader at the top drives momentum, I have also observed that there are different ways in which they do that. Sam Walton was a dynamic larger-than-life Accelerator Leader who was the consummate cheerleader. He had other leaders who reflected his leadership style like Jack Shewmaker and Don Soderquist. His immediate successor, David Glass, did not fit this mold. David as CEO was very passionate about the company, thoughtful, analytical, and disciplined. He was not the cheerleader. He did, however, tap into Don Soderquist's cheerleading ability to help him build momentum.

Len Roberts was another CEO example of sheer energy and enthusiasm who built momentum. Len brought Radio Shack to its all-time peak. His shoes were very hard to fill. Kemmons Wilson was a fireball of a leader. He was larger than life; full of energy and enthusiasm; and full of great stories and sayings like, "In business you only have to work half a day to be successful. You decide which twelve hours it is," and "There are two ways to get to the top of an oak tree: you can plant a seed, sit on it and wait until it grows up, or you can go find an oak tree and climb it. My advice is get off your rear and go climb the tree."

David Bernauer and Doug Conant are two CEOs I mentioned earlier in the "Bring Your Passion" portion of this book. Even though they are not flamboyant, they lead with passion and commitment. David led Walgreen's to become a national chain with a store on almost every corner in America, much as Kemmons Wilson had done with a Holiday Inn at every interstate exchange. Doug led Campbell's through a major turnaround and gained acclaim as one of the top CEOs of this generation.

The methods may vary, but the constant is the commitment to build momentum. That means to not just settle for good, but to always move the organization forward, even if that means occasionally taking a step or two backwards to get in the right place to accelerate and build momentum.

No matter how good a motivator the coach is in the locker room or the quarterback is in the huddle, **momentum comes from winning**. Accelerator Leaders, whether cheerleaders or quiet, thoughtful souls, create momentum by setting up their people and organizations to win. They set big goals, but inside those are smaller, winnable goals. Each time they score, they celebrate. The more they score and celebrate, the faster the next score and celebration comes. As the pace of victory increases, the momentum builds. Accelerator Leaders create momentum by changing the pitch of the river to control the pace and level of celebration of the victories. To build momentum, the victories and celebrations have to be real and genuine. Fake victories for the sake of hollow cheers kill momentum. Random celebrations for false victories kill momentum.

Similar to your personal journey, organizations need to have goals that keep them moving forward. Setting the goals that move the organization in the right direction, toward progress and impact, is critical. For many years at

Enactus, we measured the success of our program by the number of universities and colleges that joined. When we expanded internationally, it was the number of countries that also mattered. The logic behind this was that our impact involved developing students into better leaders by empowering them to improve others' lives through free enterprise. We assumed that the more institutions and students who were engaged, the greater the impact. It seemed logical. The board even used these two numbers to set our incentive goals.

Then in a meeting, a potential donor asked what our impact was. I gave him the standard answer—an increase in the number of schools and countries year after year. Instead of the usual WOW! I got, "What does that mean? How many students do you have in total? How many lives are they changing in total?" I was embarrassed because we didn't have either number. We didn't even have a mechanism to collect this data.

I went back to my team and asked the same questions and got the same response I had given. We all then realized that we were breaking our backs and, at times, breaking the bank to chase numbers that didn't accurately reflect our desired impact. Did it really make sense that adding Malta with one university counted the same in our goals as adding China with thousands of universities? Did it really make sense that adding a new university to the roster with two or three students counted more than doubling the number of students at an existing member school? Did it make sense that we didn't even measure the number of people whose lives were being changed?

We went back and did our research to find out that the number of students per campus and per country were much smaller than we thought and that the impact they were having was actually more people than we thought. We then dug deeper and realized that we could have a greater impact by using two main metrics: number of active students and number of people whose lives were improved. We then determined that once we reached a certain level of scale in the number of schools in a country, we could grow our impact faster and larger by focusing on growing the number of students per campus. That increased the number of people impacted more than just the number of campuses enrolled.

The original measurement created movement, but no real momentum toward our impact. The new metrics created momentum in the right direction. This helped us significantly to make more university students into better leaders and to improve more people's lives through entrepreneurial action.

If your organization is fighting negative momentum, set the right goals and then find a small, winnable challenge that moves you back in the right direction. Win the victory and then celebrate like crazy. Then repeat.

Momentum is also created by finding more and new water. Inside every river are springs that bubble up with fresh water to add volume and new life. Every stream eventually flows into another stream and into a river. Find those new streams that need to be added. They, too, add more volume and speed. Your organization needs a culture and river-life that constantly finds new springs and streams and is designed to absorb them into your flow. You need a method of fast assimilation of new energy.

In adding new streams, you must also have a system that determines whether a new stream is the right fit to build momentum and to add volume. It is a major challenge to combine two streams' cultures, systems and people. Over my career, I've been a close observer of a significant number of mergers and acquisitions. None of them went as planned or as smoothly as either organization thought it would. None of them. My observation is that those who approached it with eyes wide open and a bit of skepticism, were more successful than those who only looked at the potential upside and saw a bed of roses – they missed the thorns. Mergers and acquisitions should be treated more like arranged marriages than falling-in-love marriages.

One of the most difficult decisions for many organizations is to determine when it's time to be absorbed. In the non-profit sector that I know best, there have been a significant number of nonprofit startups over the last decade. They were usually started by a person who had a great passion for a specific cause, usually with a very personal connection. Many were started without looking around to see who else was serving that same cause. They pop up. Some grow, some don't. Some get to the point of realizing that the cause is better served by joining forces with another organization than fighting the fight alone. Unfortunately, it's usually the egos of the people in the organization that prevent them from making the right decision. I have seen this lead to many organizations going under, rather than joining forces. The challenge is the same in the profit sector. **Most companies reach a point of growth where they have to decide whether they should keep fighting alone or merge into a bigger river.** When this time comes, egos need to be set aside. That seldom happens.

As Enactus continued to expand to many countries, we learned to look at the landscape in a country for an existing organization with whom we could partner. Because our system relied on local engagement and allowed much local control, we found partners in several countries who had strong national programs, yet no global affiliation. By joining our network, they found the added global connection that helped them grow faster nationally. By giving up a little control, they gained in impact. This wasn't always easy and smooth. Egos, including my own, too often got in the way. When we did the right thing for the right reason – better impact – everyone won.

WHAT ABOUT THE FLOODS?

We have all seen, in person or on video, massive floods of rivers. In my teens, I saw the Mississippi at flood stage below where the Missouri and Ohio, also at flood stage, had been absorbed. The bridge over the Mississippi was covered, and my parents were on the other side. I had to wait two days for the water to go down to be reunited. The amount of water and the speed it traveled was amazing.

Rivers flood for two reasons: 1. Something blocked its path, causing a temporary dam effect; or 2. The inflows were abnormally high. In either case, flooding is caused by a lack of capacity. There is too much water for the bedrock and banks to hold it in, so it pushes outside of the river banks and overflows to the contiguous land, bringing its silt and mud with it.

In your organization, there will be times when your inflows exceed your capacity. But life happens. You add a new stream that you think will add to your flow but you find out its culture doesn't match yours. The resistance in both ecosystems creates a temporary dam. This causes a slow down or back-up of flood water. The economy changes; you get hit by a new stream out of nowhere; you get flooded. The ongoing challenge is to grow capacity at the right pace. It is difficult, and it's a catch-22: You need money to hire more people, but you need the people to bring in more funds. **Resource needs change just as everything else is fluid. You need to balance these needs constantly and be ever watchful.**

The first reality is that every river has a floodplain. Because of its fluid nature, a river's ecosystem actually extends beyond its normal banks into the floodplain, where nature and the environment push it. Your organization is built in the same way. You need to build your organization, knowing that at times you will overflow into the floodplain. You need financial reserves, fluid hiring practices, flexible logistics, and much more. Start by knowing a flood will come and recognize your floodplain.

If you think you've accomplished the perfect match between capacity and opportunity, you are deluding yourself. If you think you can build a dam and create a reservoir to end all floods, you're just like those who claimed that

World War I would be the war to end all wars. The flood is just around the corner.

The mighty rivers of the world—Nile, Amazon, Yellow, Yangtze, Volga, Danube, Ganges and Mississippi—have survived for thousands of years. They start at their headwaters and follow gravity to the sea or the ocean. Growing in size and power, they merge with other streams and are refreshed by new springs. At times, they flood, spilling over their banks, but eventually return to their original banks. All along their journey, they bring new life and renewal. Build a river not a reservoir.

SUMMARY:

- ☞ Accelerator Leaders create the momentum they need to build their rivers and maximize their impact. There are many ways they can do this, as long as they make a commitment to keep moving the organization forward.
- ☞ Momentum comes from winning. Accelerator Leaders set up their organizations and people to win.
- ☞ If your organization is fighting negative momentum, set the right goals and find a small, winnable challenge that moves you in the right direction.
- ☞ Momentum can also be created by finding and adding more water. In adding new streams, you must have a system that determines if a new stream is the right fit to build momentum and to add volume.

- ☞ Most companies reach a point where the
  to decide to join forces or to keep movir
  ward on their own. When this time comes
  need to be set aside.
- ☞ Constantly balance your needs and your ca_l
  for growth. If you think you have the perfec
  ance, check again. The flood is right aroun
  corner.

ACTION STEPS:

- ☞ Evaluate the momentum of your organizat
  from the Everglades' slow-moving swamp t
  roaring river at flood stage.
- ☞ Identify where you need to increase the mome
  tum towards desired impact and create goals th
  allow you and your team to have repeated wins
- ☞ Celebrate all of your wins that achieve the desire
  impact.
- ☞ Identify where there may be negative momen
  tum. Determine whether that "stream" can b
  turned around or if it needs to be shut off. If it
  can be turned around, identify a valuable win
  that can be achieved quickly and easily, and
  begin moving in the right direction.
- ☞ Identify in your organization the internal springs
  that are pumping new water into your river.
  Identify those new external streams that should
  be added.

🔊 Evaluate your infrastructure and the capacity of the systems, processes, and people. Determine whether they are designed and being used to enhance the flow of the river or to create dams that interfere with progress. Blow up those that are becoming dams.

CHAPTER SIXTEEN

IGNITE CHANGE.

CHANGE IS INEVITABLE. LIKE FIRE, IT CAN BE YOUR FRIEND OR YOUR ENEMY.

It might seem odd to leave the analogy of the river and water and move, instead, to fire to discuss change. But this shift does illustrate how abrupt change can be.

Visualize the scene that I experienced recently. I'm sitting on my little hobby farmer tractor at the edge of a big field. Four hundred yards away I see fire in the grass, moving rapidly in my direction. Two hundred yards in front of me is a big stand of red cedar trees that range in size from 10 to 40 feet in height. As that fire rages towards me, it ignites the cedar trees. Cedar trees have a lot of oil in their needles, and when they catch on fire, they light up like Roman candles. The flames are shooting as high as 50 to 80 feet in the air. At just 200 yards away, the heat is so intense on my face that I'm about ready to turn and drive away. What do you think my number one emotion was? Fear? Fight or flight? Nope.

My emotion was sheer exhilaration.

I was fist pumping in the air. My plan was working. The cedar trees exploded and erupted, and after just 20 minutes of being on fire, they died. The flame had been moving my way when it hit the trees, but between me and the trees there was nothing but a previously burned space. There was no more fuel to feed the flames. What had been a burning inferno was now nothing but whimpering sparks. I was elated because I had just executed a perfect controlled burn. Yes, I burned those trees on purpose.

Controlled burns are a part of the management plan for my little farm. They allow me to maximize the capacity to grow wildlife like deer, turkeys, rabbits, squirrels, and quail. The red cedar is an invasive species in my part of the country. When it takes over, it grows into a very thick grove of many trees. Because of the thick cover this creates, the red cedars kill everything below them. Nothing can grow beneath them, not grass or weeds or any other food necessary for the wildlife. The trees themselves are not good for animals to eat, nor do they grow any fruit or nut that is useful. While a red cedar grove looks nice and green all year long, it creates a wildlife food-desert.

My goal was to get rid of the red cedars so the sunlight could hit the ground and grow food for the wildlife. I could spend weeks and months with a chainsaw, cutting them down, or I could light a fire and have it all cleared in an hour. Fire is also necessary for the grass to recover and grow strong. Fire heats up the ground and releases seeds from native grasses and plants that have been dormant for years. The choice was clear: do a controlled burn.

Fire has always fascinated, but also scares me. Have you noticed that Smokey the Bear has changed his slogan? Originally it was, "Only you can prevent forest fires." Now it is, "Only you can prevent wild fires." The Forest Service changed the slogan because, in their management of all the land under their jurisdiction, they realized that fire can, in fact, be a valuable tool to properly manage forests. There is one big difference between a controlled burn and a wildfire: you carefully plan a controlled burn.

I also do controlled burns in the woods surrounding my house every few years. These controlled burns allow me to burn off the excess buildup of dead trees, fallen limbs and piles of leaves left by nature. Doing a controlled burn on my timing eliminates fuel for a fire and eliminates any risk of a wildfire caused by a lightning strike or a careless neighbor, that might destroy my home. The Forest Service does the same thing with its larger forests. Controlled burns of smaller parcels at the right time and under the right conditions significantly reduce the danger that a massive wildfire might destroy vast forests.

When I bought my farm to build my final house, I had the local conservation agent do a survey. The good news was that I had a decent stand of native warm-season grass. It looked to be a remnant of the original prairie grass that had been the dominant ecosystem 150 years ago and was paired with a very good stand of hardwood forest. When

I asked what was the best thing I could do to enhance my new property and make it a paradise for wildlife, his response surprised me. "Burn it. Burn it all."

What we have learned is that God created prairie grass in such a way that it needs to be burned about every three years, as do hardwood forests. We humans have changed the natural order because we fear fire and want to prevent natural burns from lighting strikes and careless humans. However, this results in a buildup of fuel for fires so that when there is a wildfire, it does more damage than good. A controlled burn eliminates this dangerous fuel and works with the natural cycles of grasses and forests to open the ground up for new seeds to get sunlight and grow.

Native plant species have oils that need to be burned and most of their "being" is in their deep roots. Native trees have thick bark and deep roots that can withstand fire. The invasive cedar trees have shallow roots, thin bark, and burn away quickly. A controlled burn enables the release of seeds that have been waiting for years to germinate and grow. It lets the deeply rooted plants get the sunshine they need. A controlled burn is also better for wildlife, because it's done in sections so that the wildlife can safely move away from the fire into a non-burn zone. Then they move back in a matter of days after the fire is out to enjoy fresh, green food.

This made sense, but I didn't know how to control fire or do a prescribed burn. Fortunately, my good friend Peter Layton, a Wall Street wizard, also had a company that restored prairie grass. Peter and his crew came to my farm three years in a row, did controlled burns, and taught me how to do them myself.

Fire requires fuel, oxygen, and an ignitor. It's the three-thing formula. Fire can be contained in a controlled environment. The engine in your car is a controlled burn. A specific amount of fuel, in the form of gasoline, combines with a specific amount of oxygen and is ignited by the spark of your spark plug, all inside a very heavy and strong steel cylinder. Fire in a highly-controlled environment is very safe and predictable.

What makes fire unpredictable and dangerous is not the fire, but the environment. Outside of a highly controlled environment, like the cylinder in your car engine, the three factors hit many variables. The fuel can change. Each species of wood burns at a different rate. The moisture content of the wood changes. Leaves burn differently than wood. Dry grass vs. wet grass. Short grass vs. tall grass. Oxygen is delivered by the air, and every change in humidity, wind speed and wind direction affects the burn rate of the fuel and the direction of the burn.

From Peter and his crew chief, I learned that a controlled burn requires a lot of planning and a clear understanding that the conditions and environment may change the plan. You must be equipped mentally and physically to react quickly and correctly to the changing environment, or the productive, controlled burn becomes a destructive wildfire.

These burns require controlling the conditions as much as possible. The weather and wind have to be right. Too much wind or too little humidity makes the fire hard to control, so the burn must be postponed until weather conditions are just right. First, the area requires preparation. You must make sure the entire perimeter of the area being burned has a firebreak of some kind. On my farm, this meant using natural firebreaks like creeks full of water. When fire hits water, the fuel is gone and the fire dies. Driveways and roads made of dirt or rock also make good firebreaks.

Where there are no natural firebreaks, you make them. This requires mowing the grass very low and then disking or plowing so that dirt is exposed. When the conditions are right, and you've prepared the land with firebreaks, you do a small test burn.

First, you drop the match. Actually, you use a special torch made of brass filled with the right fuel mix. The fuel is one-third gasoline and two-thirds diesel. Gasoline alone is too flammable. Diesel alone is not flammable enough. Mixed together in the right combination, they are just right and make a jelly-like liquid so you can control the drip torch. Common sense would tell you to start the fire with the wind at your back, so the wind will carry the fire forward. However, you start the fire with the wind in your face, so the fire begins to burn into the wind slowly, in a more controlled manner, consuming fuel as it goes. Once this fire has burned far enough to greatly expand your fire breaks, you then light it with the wind at your back and let the wind carry it forward.

The fire has to be monitored constantly. If you break for lunch and go inside to let it burn, you're asking for trouble. If the fuel it hits is different than you planned, it might burn hotter and higher than expected, reaching tree branches you don't want to have burned or throwing sparks so high that they go over your firebreaks. If the wind changes direction or speed, you have to react immediately, so the fire is controlled as much as possible. You have to carry water to douse it, have rakes or other tools to remove the fuel, and a torch in case you have to fight the fire with fire.

It's amazing to see how fast and how hot a fire can burn, even on a few acres. You can watch a wind gust hit and see that added oxygen can make a fire move twice as fast and go twice as high as it was just seconds ago. You walk in the wake of the fire and realize that once the fuel is gone, most of the fire is gone as well. At the frontline, it is hot and high, but just ten feet behind the line, the fire is dead. But it's not totally dead. After the main fire moves through, you have to go behind and do clean up. Soak that old stump that just won't go out. Burn that little spot of grass that somehow didn't get hit, but now needs to go under control vs. becoming a hazard later. Finally, at the end, pray for rain to quench all the embers.

If you controlled what you could; watched with vigilance; adapted quickly; and acted rapidly, you will have constructed a successful burn that will make your land much more productive. In just a few days and weeks, the blackened earth will become green, with new vegetation growing bigger and stronger than it would have without the fire. The massive amounts of oxygen released, more than makes up for the carbon dioxide released in the burn.

If you do not control the burn, it goes wild and becomes destructive. If it jumps your firebreaks, you could lose your house, car, barn, shed, and wanted trees. Worst case scenario, it could move to your neighbors' property and beyond, spreading destruction.

Change is like fire. It can be friend or foe, productive or destructive. It depends on how you and your organization deal with it. One big difference is that there is no place I know where change can be locked down like in an automobile engine cylinder. Change will happen. The flames will be constantly affected by the environment—fuel, wind, and the spark. To make change your friend, you must control what you can, through preparation and through understanding the environment. Build a culture that is vigilant, reacts quickly, and has the right tools and knowledge to take advantage of the inevitable change. If you do not manage change, it becomes a wildfire. Your enemy will burn you up.

To get in front of change, you need to do controlled burns. To do controlled burns, you need careful planning and preparation.

GET THE RIGHT EQUIPMENT.

Before you do anything, make sure you have the right equipment, both to create firebreaks and to control the fire. In your organization, make sure you have the resources you need lined up and ready to go before conducting a controlled burn. This merits careful thought since those resources are different in each organization. They will involve people, money, and political capital.

CREATE FIREBREAKS.

The firebreaks are those parameters that you will not let the controlled burn cross over. Your core values are your firebreaks. You make sure that whatever change you ignite will not violate your core values. You also make sure all your people know that your core values are your firebreaks. Firebreaks require complete removal of fire risk. No fuel of any kind can remain. Your core values must be very clear to everyone in the organization; understood by everyone; and followed by everyone. Make sure this is true before you start dropping matches.

NEXT, YOU NEED TO ASSESS THE ENVIRONMENT.

You probably already know where the dead wood and dry debris exists. What are the processes, systems, traditions, products, etc. that need to go? Like my cedar trees, they might look pretty and green, but you know they have created a food-desert. They've killed good ideas and ruined your impact. How thick is it? How fast will it burn? Will it burn and change quickly or be a slow burn? Some dead wood burns faster than others. Some changes take longer than others.

What direction is the wind moving? Swirling winds are the most unpredictable and, therefore, the most dangerous. If you light a fire in a swirling wind, it may soon turn back on you or burn in a direction you did not plan. Is your organization operating with everyone moving in the same direction, following your mission and vision, and seeking the same impact? Or are they swirling in different directions, maybe even moving to and fro? Stop the swirling and get the organization aligned and moving in the same direction before you drop any matches.

What is the wind's velocity? If there's too much wind, the fire can jump over your firebreaks or carry the sparks for miles. If there's not enough wind, the fire goes nowhere. It burns so slowly that the change takes too long. Wind speed is the mood or emotional state of the organization. If your people don't see any need for change and don't see any change coming, they are the same as a zero wind speed. The amount of effort to make change prevents the change from happening.

If your people see change happening all around the environment and feel that it is moving too fast, that rapid change may "swamp" them. They are living in fear of the unknown. They fear any change. They are like a fast-blowing wind: any little spark of internal change makes them panic. Their fears push them over the fire breaks. Rumors spread like wildfire. Flames get too hot, and the wind carries the sparks far beyond where they should. Résumés start flying like the wind. You must assess your organization and understand the wind velocity.

You will likely find different parts of the organization and different people have varied velocities. Your communications, and those of your leadership, need to be such that those with no velocity understand the need for change. You can use that same communication to calm those at high velocity by letting them know that you are going to make changes and not be a victim of change. When you get the wind velocity within range, you're almost ready to drop some matches. For my farm-controlled burns, I need a wind velocity between 3 – 8 mph. If the forecast is not within that range, I don't drop any matches.

How's the humidity in the atmosphere? No organization operates in a vacuum. You need to look at the atmosphere around you. For a controlled burn, humidity is important. If there is too much moisture in the air, the fuel will not burn or will burn too slowly to get the job done. If the air is too dry and there is no humidity, the fuel will burn much faster than planned. You have to gauge the attitude/humidity of your external atmosphere, just as you have to gauge the internal wind velocity. Who is in your atmosphere? Customers, investors, competition, media, regulators, and the public at large. How will they see a controlled burn? Will they think it's a wildfire? Will they ignore it, or will it cause panic?

Just as with wind velocity, your control mechanism within the atmosphere is good communication. Communicate clearly the need for change at the right pace and telegraph that there will be some test burns. Some will work, and some won't. You cannot hide a controlled burn. The smallest amount of smoke and flame will be seen for miles. For my farm-controlled burns, I call the local fire department and tell them what I'm doing. This lets them know not to panic if a neighbor calls. It also puts them on alert so that if my fire does go wild and I have to call them for help, they know who I am and where I live.

NOW YOU ARE READY TO DROP A MATCH.

The first match is for a test fire of a very small space with secure firebreaks. You light it up and watch to see if your evaluation of the conditions is correct. Then do another test and then another. In your organization, you do the same. Isolate one area or department. Do a test burn. Make changes. Watch to see if the conditions and outcomes are as expected. Then conduct another small test and then another.

When the tests tell you the conditions are right, you drop some matches in the main fire zone. Be careful to do this at a firebreak on the downwind side of the fire, so that the fire burns into the wind, not with the wind. Watch this fire as it grows. Constantly check to make sure the conditions haven't changed too drastically and that the outcome you wanted is what you are getting. You're not only doing a burn and creating change, you are also changing the conditions and preparing the ground for the big fire. By burning first into the wind, you are burning the fuel and making an even bigger firebreak that will prevent the big fire from going wild. Do the same in your organization. Start making changes in the main part of the operation, but do it slowly and gradually, constantly testing the conditions and outcomes. By doing it this way, you are burning up bad fuel and building a larger firebreak. You are preparing the environment for the really big burn.

Conditions are right: Equipment, check. Firebreaks, check. Wind velocity, check. Atmosphere, check. Test fires, check. Upwind burn, check.

DROP THE BIG MATCH.

You use the torch to light a line of fire all along the firebreak on the upwind side of the fire with the wind at your back. The wind will drive the fire fast and hot, blowing it right into the fuel. With the right wind and humidity, it will take on a life of its own and sweep through the entire fire zone. It will get very hot very fast and then die out quickly. The change will be made. The old built up deadwood will be gone. New growth will begin almost immediately. Future wildfires will have been prevented.

The pace between controlled burns depends on the pace of the organization and the environment. If you burn too often, the new growth doesn't get to come to fruition, and you burn what didn't need to be burned. If you burn too seldom, you become susceptible to wildfire. When Peter came down each year with his full crew and all of their equipment, we burned all 120 acres in a couple of days. They were master guides who taught me how to do controlled burns. The first year I did a burn on my own without a full crew and all the right equipment, my fire almost went wild – I put it out, but I wore myself out moving from one forefront to the next. It could have gotten really ugly.

From that experience, I learned my lesson. As I developed my farm, I made trails and planted food plots that became permanent firebreaks. I also realized that parts of my farm needed to be burned at different intervals. Now, instead of doing a controlled burn of the entire farm every three years, I do controlled burns every year of smaller 1 -10-acre parcels in the frequency each needs and during the season when they need it. In your organization, you can build a culture of doing small controlled burns regularly, as needed in each area. This will keep the deadwood from accumulating; it will keep the new growth coming; and it will prevent wildfires.

The biggest fire I set at Enactus was the name change from SIFE (Students In Free Enterprise) to Enactus. When I became the CEO of Students In Free Enterprise in its 7th year, it had already become known as SIFE. SIFE and the Statue of Liberty were prominent in the logo and on other materials. Marketing was always a part of our three-year strategic plans. Every time we launched a new plan, the board would bring up the need to change the name, as SIFE always required explanation. Students In Free Enterprise was a name longer than most people wanted to say.

During one of these early planning meetings, one of our board members was very assertive about the need for a name change and volunteered to lead a task force to explore that option. At the first task force meeting, he announced that he had asked for the establishment of the task force to approve what he considered was the obvious choice for a new name. He shared his perfect name. The task force all nodded in agreement. However, that name was already being used by another organization much older than ours. The chairman of the task force was deflated, and the task force was dissolved. The issue of a name change, however, did not go away.

The issue of the name change continued to resurface every time a new marketing campaign was launched. Instead of a name change, we usually ended up changing the logo. As a result, I have a collection of pins and shirts with more than a dozen different logos that we used in my 34-year career. If you're changing your logo with that type of frequency, it's a sign that there is a deeper issue.

With the expansion into more and more countries and different languages, the name continued to be an issue. In many countries, "Students In Free Enterprise" did not translate well, or at all. The two-word phrase "Free Enterprise" is very American and Anglo. While there is some disagreement on what these two words mean in America, most Americans know what is meant when these two words are combined. In some countries, two words had to be pieced together to try and make it work.

In one developing country, students were holding a free enterprise conference and had gathered a very large crowd. After the program began, the crowd got very restless; then very agitated; and then very angry, until there was almost a riot. Because of the local words used by the students to say Free Enterprise, the people attending the event thought they were going to receive a Free Business that they could then take home and make money! As a consequence of the translation challenge with the phrase Free Enterprise, most countries used the acronym SIFE. When asked what it meant, many of them would insert their own words like Students In Future Economy or Success Is For Everyone or they would use native words that matched the letters SIFE. The result was a branding nightmare.

While going through our strategic planning process, the name issue came up again. I was approaching my 30th anniversary as CEO and the reality hit me that I would not be there forever. As I thought through what needed to be done to prepare for a succession plan, I came to the conclusion that I was the one who had to address the name issue. We had to resolve, once and for all, what the name would be going forward. I hoped I had the political capital to force a decision, but knew the next CEO would be new and would not have such political capital. I also remembered the unsuccessful processes from the past, including almost every new board member doodling during the board name discussion and handing me their version of the perfect logo. All of them owned, or were senior executives, at large companies who had paid millions of dollars to design logos, but for us, their doodles were golden.

The board agreed to let management secure an agency to help with this process. Mat Burton was our chief marketing officer. He did due diligence in looking for the right agency to help us with this process. When he went to the meeting to pitch the process, he opened with, "You've probably never heard of us." He was interrupted by one of the agency team members who said, "I know all about SIFE. I was one of the students on the SIFE Champions from Poland who presented at the first World Cup."

Mat was now relieved and went on to tell them our need. When Mat told me the story, I knew this was the right choice. The board agreed. At the board meeting, the agency said they would do extensive research, both inside and outside our network. The board asked them to consider all the options discussed above and they agreed. Then they asked, "Are you open to considering a completely new name?" The board discussed it and decided they would consider a new name. However, the agency needed to know that changing the name was the last option, with only a longshot at getting approval. All of us on the management team, including Mat, agreed with the board 100% on this.

Mat and the agency began the research. I began preparations for a controlled burn change. We began communicating to all the countries' leadership and boards the importance and value of a consistent global brand. We communicated that we had retained this agency and that they would bring their recommendation in to the board. We also communicated that once the board made its decision, we would enforce the branding standard requirements in all the contracts we had with each country.

I knew that the timing was right because Doug McMillon, the CEO of Walmart International, was chairman of the SIFE board. Walmart was our largest and most long-term donor. I knew that if Doug supported this naming decision, it would encourage other donors to see the value as well.

The agency did their due diligence and extensive research. Mat made sure they received input from all facets of our network: students, faculty, country leaders, board members, and donors. They also did an excellent job of determining our market position and name recognition outside our network.

They reported their findings to the leadership team. Inside the network, there were high levels of approval from every segment of the network, and high levels of name recognition. This, of course, made us gloat a bit. Outside the network, very low levels of name recognition were found.

This was what we expected and why we knew we needed a stronger marketing effort. They reported that while every segment of the network loved what we did, very few loved or even really liked the name. They also reported that when people outside the network heard what we did, without using any name, there was a high degree of interest in joining us. But, when they told the same story using any version of our current name, it caused confusion and received less interest. The full name made some sense to some, but "SIFE" made no sense to anyone and just confused them.

The evidence was overwhelming. Finding a new name was the right thing for the organization. At first, all of us on the leadership team felt gut-punched. We came up with every argument as to why this wasn't right and why we couldn't make it happen. The more we talked, the more we knew the research data was right. We all agreed that we needed to take a recommendation to the board to consider a name change. I knew I would need a much bigger match.

My firebreaks weren't large enough for this controlled burn. We doubled down on our communications about the importance of a global brand and added the need for making sure it was the right brand. I made a beeline to Doug McMillon's office. I knew that if exploring a name change was not acceptable to Doug and Walmart, it would not be acceptable to the rest of the board and our donors. I shared all the research with Doug. We discussed it and the ramifications. He asked, "You have been with this organization longer than anyone. You've devoted your career and life to it. Do you believe this is the right thing to do for the long-term good of the organization?"

"Yes, I do, and now is the time to do it," I replied.

"Walmart and I support the organization because of what you do, not because of your name. You have my support conditional on finding a new name we can all support."

Early in my career, Jack Shewmaker and Bob Plaster taught me an important lesson about board meetings: Never bring in big surprises. I spent hours on the phone calling every board member, sharing the information and recommendation. At the board meeting, the discussion was very intense and at times, very heated. Ultimately, the board decided unanimously to support the recommendation from the leadership and the agency to explore a new name. The agency conducted more research and also discovered that while SIFE is not a word in English, in some countries it actually was a word. In one country it meant "to die," in another it meant "sword," and in some it was a very vulgar word. Once this was shared with the board, they approved letting the network know that we were going to change the name. The sentiment of the board and leadership was to avoid using an acronym or creating a new word.

Once it was announced, our firebreaks were tested at all levels within all segments of the organization. Suddenly, people who had told me for years that they didn't really like our name became passionate about not changing it – including the guy who led the name change task force 10 years earlier. We made hundreds of calls and held hundreds of meetings. By sharing the data and the case for change, we had moved the network from a "No way. We don't want a name change," to "Okay, we'll think about it." Many had moved to full agreement of the need for a name change, but they had concerns about the cost and proper execution of a name change.

While I was expanding the firebreaks, Mat and the agency went to work to find our new name. They began their search, based on their research, telling how the network described us. As part of the process, they also asked everyone in the network to submit their suggestions. This process created 8,000 options. Seventy-five percent of these disappeared as a result of a cursory trademark search in the USA. Seventy-five percent of those remaining disappeared with a cursory global trademark search. The list was now narrowed down to a few hundred potential names. Most of the names using real words had failed the trademark test. We were now required to look more closely at newly created words.

After using the filter of determining how the remaining candidate names would translate into the primary languages in the network, we were down to a few hundred. Mat and the agency got this list down to about 30. This list was taken to the board and initially rejected. There was no one name that everyone could agree on. Several suggested that we abandon the effort; go back to the original name; and find a way to make that work. A few actually began offering new names they had just doodled. Chairman McMillon asked the board to force rank the top 12 so that the leadership could narrow it down further for the next meeting.

Mat, the agency, and the leadership team went to work narrowing the field. These discussions were always intense and often got heated. I remember pulling over to a parking lot in a small town on my way to the office. I was on a call with Mat and was about to lose my signal, driving in the Ozark Mountains. The day before, Mat had given me his and the agency's top three choices, making a very strong case for their number one choice. It was the only made-up word of the three choices. I had made it very clear that I didn't want a made-up name, but the trademark and translation challenges had forced me to consider it. This new word was just sitting there with not much explanation around it.

I hadn't slept at all that night, thinking about the name change and the leadership team meeting the next morning. "Mat, I've given much thought and prayer about the recommended name. As you know from some of our heated discussions, I was not originally fond of this name. However, when I boiled down what we do, I think it is best described as using entrepreneurial action to improve peoples' lives. Using the concept of Entrepreneurial Action for all of Us, the proposed name Enactus now makes sense. It is the right name." Mat shared the concept behind the Enactus name, and the leadership team agreed.

My struggle wasn't with a name change or any of the choices. My struggle was that I had seen "improving lives through free enterprise" as my impact, my calling. I had to come to terms with the reality that the words I used to express my impact were not universally understood. The name and mission of the organization I led needed to be universally understood. I had not yet found the words that fit until we came up with "Entrepreneurial Action that enables real human progress." Entrepreneurial action embodied entrepreneurship, market economics, business, personal responsibility, freedom of choice, and financial discipline—all the things that I saw as being free enterprise. I finally felt like we had found a name that would let us share our mission in a universal language.

We took the three final candidate names to the board. We shared the first two. One had already fallen out, as the week before the meeting, one of the candidates for President of the United States had announced it as his campaign theme. We were flattered that we had come up with a good idea. But we were also relieved that the board would know that announcing that name as our new name was not an option at that time. We shared the second name and the rationale behind it. Mat then made a great presentation explaining how we were all about entrepreneurial action that enabled real human progress. He then unveiled the Enactus name choice. Backed by this concept, the board unanimously agreed. The next step was approval of a logo, which was not an easy process, but Mat, his team, and the agency delivered what the leadership team and the board approved unanimously. Adding the unfinished origami graphic to the name made a perfect logo.

Once we had announced to the network that the board had voted to change the name and had asked the entire network for name recommendations, we sequestered the process. We didn't want to let all 8,000 proposed names out. Names might gain interest, only to discover that they couldn't be used because of trademark issues. Internally, we limited this project to only the marketing team, the leadership team, and the board. We even kept the marketing department locked away and off limits to any other associate. We managed to keep all the proposed names confidential inside this circle until final board approval.

We were now ready to drop the big match at the World Cup competition in Washington, D.C. We started at the all-country staff dinner. We swore them to secrecy, showed the presentation and got strong support. The next day, we went to the council of country board chairs. We swore them to secrecy as well. We also got strong support from this group. The presentation was a slide show explaining how we derived the name, followed by a beautiful video explaining who we were. The video ended with "We are Enactus!" That evening, it was time for the big show.

We were about to drop the last and biggest match, the unveiling of the new name at the end of the opening ceremony. Mat and the agency felt that the best way to introduce it was to show the video. It was great, and I agreed. I set the stage a bit and then showed the video. The response in the auditorium was okay, but not great. The response from the audience watching online was not good. Our social media lit up strongly negative. Our firebreaks were being severely challenged. We were about to have a social media wildfire and our new name was about to be rejected by our network.

While this was going on inside the auditorium and online, the marketing team frantically worked to replace all the signage bearing the old name with the new name, logo and branding material throughout the convention center. When the students walked out of the auditorium, they walked into a convention center covered with the new logo and branding material focusing on entrepreneurial action. It was a big hit! The students started posting pictures online and taking selfies at every display of the new logo. The origami symbol was especially popular. While the firebreak held and the tide began to turn, the social media debate continued among the students and alumni.

The momentum behind the name change grew over the next few days during the World Cup. When it was time for the Final Awards Ceremony, I knew things were moving in the right direction, but I also knew the controlled burn was still capable of going wild. I left the room for several minutes, which caused a bit of a panic for those managing the event. I returned to the auditorium just in time to be introduced on stage. They were surprising me with a recognition of my 30th Anniversary as CEO. One of the recognitions announced by Chairman McMillon was that the World Cup Trophy, with the new logo attached, would be named the Alvin Rohrs Trophy. I was very touched and very honored.

After this recognition came the time when I traditionally addressed the organization. The 30th Anniversary recognition was a very humbling introduction. I began my talk in my normal pattern of telling of my experience as a student and faculty advisor. I then shared an inspirational message, as was my norm. As I began ending this message, I also began to take off my tie and then unbutton my shirt. My wife thought I was ill, maybe even having a heart attack. My son thought I had lost it and was about to come on stage to help me off.

I continued my message, "I have just shared that I've been part of this organization since I was a student in college, even before I became CEO 30 years ago. I have filled every position from student to alumnus to faculty advisor, to country leader and now Global CEO. I have devoted my life to this organization," I said as I continued to unbutton my shirt, "and no one in this room or watching online has devoted more time to it than I have. No one has more at stake in this organization than I do. I want all of you to know that I am 100% totally committed to this organization and I want all of you to know—I am Enactus."

At that same moment I pulled my shirt all the way open to reveal the Enactus logo emblazoned on the T-shirt I had snuck away to put on. The crowd went wild. Social media surged to all positive. For weeks, Enactus students posted videos online doing what became known as "The Superman Move:" opening their shirts to show the logo and shouting, "We are Enactus!" The change had been made. The fire was out, and we could already see new growth coming from the new name.

As an Accelerator Leader you must be a change agent. You must be the change. You must be able to envision the future by envisioning your organization's legacy and focusing on its true impact.

Be the change or be its victim. The choice is yours.

SUMMARY:

    ☞   Change is inevitable; it can be your friend or your enemy and it can be productive or destructive.

⇪ To get in front of change in your organization, you need to do controlled burns after careful preparation and planning.

⇪ To prepare, you need to evaluate your organization; gather the materials you need; and use your core values to create firebreaks, before dropping the initial match.

⇪ Choose to be the change or you will end up being its victim.

ACTION STEPS:

⇪ Identify one place in the organization to conduct your small-scale controlled burn.

⇪ Identify the dead wood and fuel that needs to be consumed so that new growth can happen.

⇪ Follow the instructions for firebreaks, fuel, atmosphere, temperature, and wind velocity. When the conditions are right, drop a match.

⇪ Analyze the entire organization and prioritize those areas that need controlled burns. Then begin preparations for those burns.

⇪ Prepare your organization so that it is ready for regular, controlled burns and therefore becomes an organization of change.

CONCLUSION

────●────────────────●────

CHAPTER SEVENTEEN

WILL YOUR IMPACT STAND
THE TEST OF TIME?

As I write this, the headlines of the week are that Toys R Us is closing stores across America. *Time* and *Fortune* are on the market and the owners don't expect to get much for them. Then, Charles Lazarus, founder of Toys R Us, dies at 93.

At the beginning of my career, these were all iconic brands, and I had the opportunity to meet Mr. Lazarus. Toys R Us was considered an unstoppable force in retail. *Time Magazine* was the authority on news, while making the Fortune 500 list of the largest U.S. corporations was how companies measured their success. The original

Fortune 500 list was published in 1955; only 60 of the original companies remain on the list.

If you measure your organization's success based only on money earned, buildings built, or products sold, your success will soon be gone. If you measure your success by how you changed the human condition; how you made the world better than you found it; and how you improved people's lives, then your impact and your legacy will live on beyond yourself and your organization.

I believe that only things eternal will live forever. The book of Matthew quotes Jesus as saying, "Store up for yourselves treasures in heaven, where neither moth or rust destroys, and where thieves do not break in and steal; for where your treasure is there your heart will be also."

There are examples of humankind trying to build structures on earth to reach the eternal. The Bible records the story of the Tower of Babel, where humanity tried to build a tower tall enough to reach heaven. The pyramids in Egypt were the Pharaohs' attempts. My wife and I visited the Terracotta Warriors site in China. I had seen pictures of the site and seen various renditions of the statues coming to life in movies. I didn't comprehend the full story until being there and experiencing it live.

The first realization is that only one of the statues was found intact. All the rest were in small pieces that archeologists had to painstakingly restore, like giant jigsaw puzzles. There are still hundreds underground that are continually being restored. It will take years and years before they are all finished. Each one is unique. There are no replicas. This was not mass production, but time-consuming art. There were different types and ranks of soldiers as well. The detail on each is amazing. They were buried underground for a thousand years until a small parcel farmer accidently dug one up. The excavation shows that apparently a king or ruler of some kind had the army of terracotta warriors made to either escort him to the eternal paradise or possibly even to try to conquer it upon arrival. In the least, the army of statues and the temple would be a tribute to his greatness.

There is little other evidence of the king's reign or of his belief system. There is also little evidence of how the warriors were made or by whom. What the archeologists have learned is that very shortly after his death, the temple was raided by many people; the warriors were smashed into little pieces; and the temple was set on fire. Apparently, the king's obsession with making the warriors, coupled with the process used, made the people hate the king so much that they destroyed everything he built within days of the his death. The lessons learned for me were: don't trample on people on your way to heaven and don't expect earthly structures to get you there.

Susan Alford was the head of Walmart's people division when our partnership started. Behind her desk was a plaque that read, "If you want a return in a year, grow wheat. If you want a return in 10 years, grow trees. If you want a return in 100 years, grow people."

Make sure that your impact is on people, not things, and it will survive you. It can even ripple throughout generations.

Will the organization that I led for 34 years live forever? When I announced my retirement the organization had lots of positive momentum and a strong balance sheet. I'm sure it will prosper, but not last forever. Will my legacy last beyond my time on earth? Maybe. Recently a dear friend sent me a magazine article that featured his son winning the outstanding teacher award in the business school at Ole Miss. In the article, his son explained how his time in SIFE, now Enactus, had given him the opportunity to teach others about free market economics and how that had inspired him to become a teacher.

This year I connected to an Enactus alumna who had been selected by the U.S. State Department, as one of only 500 Nelson Mandela Scholars, to participate in the Young African Leaders Institute (YALI) summer-long intensive leadership development program in the U.S. She would then return to Nigeria and become one of its new young leaders. She told me there were other Enactus alumni chosen as well.

There are tens of thousands of students who have been accelerated by numerous academic and business leaders, because of my work. There are millions of people in small villages and big cities whose lives were accelerated by the students. Few of those who were accelerated will know my name, but they have started a ripple effect that I believe will go on for generations.

Nelson Mandela's statesmanship and desire for reconciliation made life better for millions and inspired millions more. His life story and service to South Africa and to the world have accelerated millions of people who have courageously fought for freedom, independence, and self-reliance. He showed the world a better path than retribution and revenge. A path that, if we take it, will build a better world.

Sam Walton's desire to help people save money and live better continues to live on, from one store to thousands, and from rural America to the entire world through technology. His entrepreneurial life has also inspired millions to be courageous and risk it all to start new adventures. The millions of associates who worked for him and the customers who continue to be served by his successors have all been accelerated.

Become an Accelerator Leader. Be the change. Live a legacy.

EPILOGUE

I have had a blessed life and career. I grew up with parental role models who were committed to their faith and to serving God. That meant showing God's love to others, especially to boys in need and in trouble.

My early career thinking in high school was more focused on what I could do to make a living. As explained in earlier chapters, I wasn't going to be a craftsman of any kind, so college was the logical choice. I talked a lot, so many of my friends told me I should consider being a lawyer or politician. I enrolled at Southwest Baptist University because my sister was going there, we only had one car, and they offered me a $500 music scholarship and a minister's child scholarship.

My college advisor, Larry Whatley, encouraged me to add business to my majors since there weren't a lot of job openings for political science majors, especially if I didn't get into law school. Because he had seen my high school transcript, I understood his concern about my potential to get into law school. I had graduated fourth in my high school class, but there were only 18 of us. Yes, only 18, that's not a typo.

My intro to business class was taught by a serial entrepreneur named Bill Williams. We called him "Bill Bill." On the first day of class he asked who in the class was a Democrat, who was a Republican, and who was an Independent. After all was done, he looked at me and said, "Mr. Rohrs, you didn't raise your hand for any of the three. Why not?"

"I am a socialist," I replied.

"I'm not sure why you're in this class, but I doubt you'll be a socialist at the end of the semester," was his response.

As I attended this class, and my economics and accounting classes, I began to see the light. I entered college right after my father had been cheated by some unscrupulous businessmen. I had the attitude that all business people were evil, and profit was what businesses earned by lying, cheating, or stealing. Part of my class assignment from Bill Bill was to interview the leaders of the small town of Bolivar, Missouri, where the college was located, and to write a paper on what made Bolivar work.

I interviewed the local banker. To my surprise, he didn't have fangs or a pointed tail; he actually cared about his customers and only foreclosed on a property as a last resort, usually losing money when he did. I interviewed the president of the country's largest artificial flower maker. Again, no horns or forked tongue, only a friendly man who took good care of his workers and customers. Same thing with the restaurant owner, the other bankers, the petroleum distributor, real estate developers, car dealers, and so on.

My paper reported that Bolivar worked because of the business owners, developers, managers, and entrepreneurs who worked hard, made a profit ethically, started businesses, and created jobs. The local government was good for roads, police, and fire protection. Bill Bill didn't tell me what to think. He accelerated me by letting me explore the local community on my own. In the end, he was right: I was no longer a socialist.

I was invited by the dean of the school of business, Dr. Ed Clark, to help start and join a new organization called Students In Free Enterprise, now named Enactus. This began my long career. Through my studies, I learned that a market economy with free enterprise was the economic system that offered the most opportunity to the most people in America and in the world. I knew that free enterprise was the best path to accelerate real human progress, not only economic progress, but improved health, happiness and sustainability. Giving people the freedom to choose their own paths in life and the economic freedom to choose what they spend their hard-earned money on is the best way to accelerate economic growth and the best way to achieve sustainability. The freedom of exchange in a market economy democratizes economic decision making because the individual consumer is the king of the market. I wanted my impact to be accelerating real human progress by improving people's lives through free enterprise, business, and entrepreneurship.

As my career heated up, I received many offers in business, politics, and government. Some offers were more prestigious and higher paying than my chosen career/position. All were tempting, but I knew none would lead me to my chosen destination and fulfill my calling.

Had I taken those easier paths, my life would not be the adventure it has been, and my circle of friends would have been much smaller. I believe God has a plan for each of us, and I'm thankful for the one He gave me.

ABOUT THE AUTHOR

As Chief Accelerator Dr. Rohrs brings innovative solutions to market through his high level global connections. Innovations he has introduced to the market are in the areas of cybersecurity, environmental sustainability, corporate finance and insurance.

As President & CEO of Enactus for more than thirty years, Dr. Alvin Rohrs took a small regional nonprofit with 18 participating universities in the US and grew it into an international force for sustainable social entrepreneurship with 70,000 active students at 1700 universities in 36 countries. Working alongside the Enactus board of directors, comprising leaders from some of the world's most successful companies including Walmart, Walgreen's, Hallmark, American Greetings, KPMG, The Coca-Cola Company, PepsiCo, Campbell's, Rich Products, Unilever, Bic, Jack Link's, Newell Rubbermaid, The Hershey Company, he guided the organization to develop a coordinated approach to building sustainable Enactus programs throughout the world. Under his leadership, annual revenue increased from $100,000 to $20 million. And during that time, more than 800,000 students became entrepreneurial action leaders, and more than 18 million people worldwide were empowered to improve their livelihoods.

Widely recognized as an expert on entrepreneurship, social impact and acceleration leadership, Dr. Rohrs delivers powerful keynotes, conducts seminars and workshops, and provides consultation for companies and organizations in the business and non-profit sectors. He specializes in bringing innovative solutions to market through his high-level global connections.

A captivating storyteller, he has spoken at the United Nations Foundation Plus Social Good Summit; Festival Economia in Trento, Italy; Circulo de Economia Forum on Social Responsibility in Barcelona, Spain; and the Clinton Global Initiative in New York City. He has been a featured speaker at numerous national industry meetings including GMA (Grocery Manufacturers Association) CEO Forum, RILA (Retail Industry Leaders Association) CEO Summit and the NACDS (National Association of Chain Drug Stores) annual meeting. His media appearances include Fortune, Forbes, Inc., The Wall Street Journal, HuffingtonPost.com, Time Magazine, and Entrepreneur and was also featured in the book True Leaders by Bette Price & George Ritcheske. In addition, Dr. Rohrs has testified at U.S. Congressional hearings on financial literacy and student entrepreneurship.

An honoree in the Congressional Record three times for leadership, Dr. Rohrs received a National Charity Award in 1992, was named National "Entrepreneur of the Year, Supporter of Entrepreneurship" in 1995 by Inc.

magazine, and was chosen to be an Olympic Torch Carrier for the XIX Olympic Winter Games in Salt Lake City, UT. He earned a Juris Doctorate at the University of Missouri Columbia Law School, a Bachelor's Degree in Business from Southwest Baptist University, and was awarded an Honorary Doctorate in Business from SBU. He and his wife live in Dunnegan, Missouri, and have two grown children.